Cape Cod Maritime Disasters

A COLLECTION OF PHOTOGRAPHS OF MARITIME ACCIDENTS AROUND CAPE COD, NANTUCKET AND MARTHA'S VINEYARD.

BY WILLIAM P. QUINN

The above illustration was used in Harpers Magazine to depict the trauma of shipwreck. It was entitled: "Overturned Life-boat." This type of boat was unsinkable and it appears that the men are trying to right the boat and save themselves and their survivors.

Library of Congress Catalog Card No. 90-91663

ISBN-0-936972-13-0

Printed in the United States of America by:

Bookcrafters Incorporated, Chelsea, Michigan

Published by:

Lower Cape Publishing, P.O. Box 901, Orleans, Massachusetts 02653

Other books by
William P. Quinn

SHIPWRECKS AROUND CAPE COD (1973)
SHIPWRECKS AROUND NEW ENGLAND (1978)
SHIPWRECKS AROUND MAINE (1983
SHIPWRECKS ALONG THE ATLANTIC COAST (1988)
SHIPWRECKS IN NEW YORK WATERS (1989) co-author Paul C. Morris

PREFACE

This book is the result of seventeen years of additions to a file of old and new photographs illustrating Cape Cod maritime disasters. Since publishing the book *Shipwrecks Around Cape Cod* in 1973, the maritime traffic around the peninsula has experienced a substantial number of accidents, adding new material to an expanding collection. In addition to this was the acquisition of several previously unpublished pictures, donated by friends who have similar interests in the field. This latest work contains a variety of maritime wrecks which have occurred around the Cape and Islands. The Coast Guard has augmented their abilities in the search and rescue field with space-age technology and new procedures. When compared to yesterday's Life Saver, today's coastal vanguard is ten times as efficient because of modern techniques and the latest in communications.

The study of maritime disasters is varied and interesting. Research into old wrecks often leads to further study when additional incidents are found in the same time period. Most of the stories are found in old newspapers, or taken from microfilms which are sometimes scratched and barely readable. This data is followed up in the early maritime publications to verify the reporting. Every attempt is made to insure the authenticity of the information before it is entered in the book. Despite all of the best efforts, errors sometimes appear which, no doubt, in time, will be corrected by future publications on the subject.

Another illustration from Harpers Magazine depicting a maritime disaster with the breeches-buoy in operation rescuing survivors on deck. Rescues were usually carried out in the sea conditions depicted here but in reality they were often worse.

This book is dedicated

to my brother

HOWARD W. QUINN

Winter takes a toll on small fishing boats. Seams open and overnight a boat can sink. The next morning the owner arrives to discover a few weeks of salvage work instead of a days fishing. The lot of the Cape Cod fisherman is not a happy one. *Photo by the Author.*

CONTENTS

The line drawings in this book are by Paul C. Morris of Nantucket, Massachusetts. Mr. Morris is a noted marine painter who is also a scrimshaw artist and maritime historian.

LIST OF PHOTOGRAPHS

****

Above: The Life Saving Service had various insignia through the years. The circle on top left was used from 1848 through 1871. The life-ring at top right with the crossed boat hook and oar was used from 1872 to 1914. The Revenue Cutter Service merged with the Life Saving Service in 1915. The crossed oars on a life ring, above left, was later used as a surfman's pin. The modern Coast Guard uses the crossed anchors (above) surrounded by a rope with a shield in the center with the motto "Semper Paratus". **Below:** An early view of the United States Life Saving Service men hooking up the horse to the beach cart, probably to haul it out for a drill. The photograph was taken in Provincetown.

SHIP'S RIGGING

The legendary days of sailing ships have passed by and the sight of a full rigged ship with all sails set, with the wind on her quarter and the bone in her teeth are but a memory of yesteryear. During the early to mid 19th century, sailing ships provided the transportation for goods and people the world over. There were several types of vessels carrying a variety of rigging. Today it is difficult to understand the different rigs and what they were called. A bark was a ship but a ship was not a bark. The reason for this was that all species of vessels had the generic name of ship. To analyze this statement one has only to look at the illustrations of both vessels. A ship (rig) was a vessel with three or more masts, all of which were square rigged with yard arms running port and starboard. The three masts on a ship were called the fore, main and mizzen. The foremast was nearest the bow. The main mast was central and the mizzen was near the stern of the ship. In some ships, there were four masts. The aftermost mast was always called the spanker, no matter if there were several masts.

A bark was a vessel with three masts. The mizzen was fore and aft rigged. That is, there were no yard arms or square sails on the aftermost mast. A barkentine was a vessel of three or more masts, all fore and aft rigged, except for the foremast which was square rigged. A brig was a vessel of two masts, both of which were square rigged. A hermaphrodite brig was a vessel of two masts, however the foremast was square rigged and the mainmast was fore and aft rigged. A brigantine was also a vessel of two masts with the foremast square rigged but the main topmast was rigged with square topsails and fore and aft rigged on the main lower mast. Other square rigged vessels sailed under different names. One name was the shipantine. This was a vessel with four masts, the fore and main were square rigged and the mizzen and spanker were fore and aft rigged. Another common name for this rig was the jackass bark. There were only two of these ships under sail in the Atlantic ocean in the late 19th century. One old timer quipped that this vessel looked like a schooner chasing a brig.

A marked contrast with the square rigged ship was the schooner. A schooner was a vessel carrying a fore and main mast, both of which were fore and aft rigged. As schooners grew in size they had to be built with more than two masts. Three masted schooners appeared in the early 1800's. History relates that there were several multi-masted schooners around the early 1900's. There were four, five and six masters. The largest of them all was the Thomas H. Lawson, a giant seven masted schooner with a steel hull. Only one of this type of vessel was built. Most of the huge wooden coal schooners were built in Maine in the late 19th and early 20th century. On the Lawson, the masts were called fore, main, mizzen, jigger, driver, pusher and spanker. All of the masts carried fore and aft sails. The formula of two men to a mast, plus the Captain, resulted in economic operations of the schooners. A variation of the schooner rig was the topsail schooner. A vessel with two or more masts, all fore and aft rigged with the exception of the fore topmast which carried square topsails. Occasionally on some early topsail schooners, some square topsails were carried on the main topmast as well. The sloop was a vessel with one mast. The sloop carried only two sails, a headsail and a mainsail. It was one of the oldest styles in the maritime trade and was in use commercially the world over.

All of the ships, barks, brigs etc., carried head sails. These were triangular sails which ran from the top of the foremast to the bowsprit and jibboom and were used to help control the steering of the ship. Most of the vessels also carried staysails which were fore and aft sails rigged to stays that ran between the masts. There were other different terms used to describe sails on a ship such as the courses, topsails, topgallants and royals. Many older square rigged ships used stunsails in fair winds to increase the speed of the vessel. They were extensions of the lower square sails rigged on the ends of the yards. The days of sailing vessels have passed into history and few of the large sailing ships are left today. These are largely for ceremonial times and get underway only on special occasions. The illustrations on the following pages show the differences of the vessels described above.

Four-Masted Double-Topsail Ship

Ship

Bark

Barkentine

Brig

Hermaphrodite Brig

The standard rigging seen on sailing vessels of the 19th century is illustrated above. Square sails run port and starboard or perpendicular to the direction the ship is going. *Illustrations from U.S. List of Merchant Vessels, 1891.*

Brigantine

Schooner

Fore-and-Aft Three-Masted Schooner

Four-Masted Schooner

Schooner Pilot-Boat

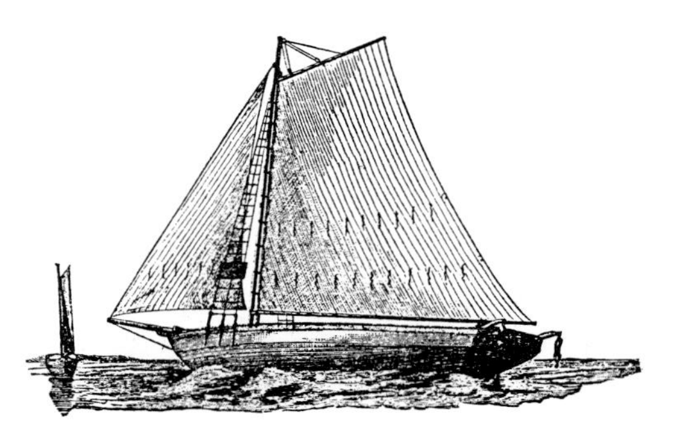

Sloop

The fore and aft rig for schooners and sloops. The popularity of this type of rigging was due to economics. It required far fewer men to operate a schooner than a brig. *Illustrations from U.S. List of Merchant Vessels, 1891.*

An illustration of the men of the Life Saving Service going to the aid of a stranded and broken vessel. The rigging is in shambles and the crew gathered in the fo'csle awaiting the surfboat. This is typical work for the Life Savers of the day.

Chapter One

The peninsula of Cape Cod, on the coast of Massachusetts, has been the curse of navigators for three hundred years. This promontory lies between the ports of Boston and New York. It was the principle route of commerce when the Pilgrims began trading with the Dutch at Fort Amersterdam (New York), in the early part of the seventeenth century. The Puritans of the Massachusetts Bay Colony established a trading post near the Manomet River. This river, later called Monument River, is now part of the Cape Cod Canal. By the use of this waterway and an overland trail, they were able to avoid the hazardous navigation around the outer shores of Cape Cod. As time passed, commerce with other settlements along the Atlantic coast developed. Cape Cod projects out into the Atlantic ocean almost forty miles, It then sweeps north for another thirty miles with rows of shifting sand bars near the coast which are moved around by the wind and ocean currents. The reefs reach out from the shore like fingers, beckoning the unwary vessels to the beach.

The ocean surrounds Cape Cod and has been important in its history. The stormy waters have terrorized the sailor, wrecked his ship, spilled out his cargoes and more often, caused his death. The tragic list of maritime disasters is not a modern phenomenon for in 1620 the Pilgrim's ship *Mayflower*, was nearly wrecked on Pollock Rip Shoals off what is now Chatham. The ship was bound for the Hudson River colony, which, at that time, was a part of northern Virginia. The early shipwrecks were most always complete disasters. It was a savage shoreline with no aid for the mariner and the loss of life was, invariably, total. The course of history has been changed many times because of maritime disasters. A sailing ship, caught in a northeast storm off the backside of Cape Cod had less than a 50-50 chance of survival. The wrecks caused much suffering from the loss of life and property. The accidents were not always storm related. Fog blinds the sailor and is the cause of collisions in crowded sealanes. Cold weather slows down human functions. Quick and immediate reactions were sometimes necessary to avoid wrecking a sailing ship. It was hard to handle stiff canvas sails when the sailor's hands were frozen and the ice coated lines could not be moved.

The most treacherous area for merchant shipping was the stormy backside of Cape Cod. The town of Truro was once called Dangerfield because of its hazardous area for maritime commerce. The inherent dangers have prevailed for over 350 years. Ships, even today, come ashore on the outer shores albeit with less frequency now than in the 18th and 19th centuries. In August of 1635, a hurricane struck Cape Cod and caused high tides and blew down thousands of trees. The annals of the Plymouth Colony reported that: "It began southeast and parted towards the south and east and veered sundry ways. The wrecks of it will remain a hundred years."

Left: The earliest shipwreck on Cape Cod is marked at Nauset Beach in Orleans along with information about the German Submarine attack during World War One. **Below:** The hull of an unidentified vessel wrecked on Nauset Beach in Orleans provides a diversion for young people to explore on a summer day in the late 1800's. *Photos courtesy of a friend.*

The geography of Cape Cod has, over the years, been altered by the sea. Each year, two or three feet, sometimes more, is eroded from the ocean beaches by the continual assault of the Atlantic. Some of the material is deposited on each end of the peninsula but much of it is carried away by the movement of the currents. The evidence of this is graphically illustrated in the early histories. From Deyo's History of Barnstable County, published in 1890:

> "The peninsular character of the Cape has distinguished it during all historic time; but it is entirely plausible that in geologic time it had a more continental character. Of the south shore of Barnstable where is now a channel two miles wide, separating Bishop and Clerk's light from the land, was once a sheep pasture through which only a small creek flowed, and within the period of our own colonial history the Nantucket farmers cut fencing on an island seven miles off Chatham, where now the rushing restless tide has undisputed sway. Ram island, where many of the present residents of Chatham have repaired for frolic and berries, has gone down in the unequal strife and the sullen sea sweeps over a spot where the Vikings dwelt eight centuries ago - the spot which was still inhabitable when in 1620, Sir Humphrey Gilbert noted it as Nauset Island. If the physical character of this peninsula has been thus modified by the Titanic war which old ocean - so old and so busy - has forever waged upon it, not less important upon its animal and vegetable life has been the effect of what Michalet, in his LaMer calls the tyranny of the sea."

This, in effect, seems to predict the ultimate consumption, by the ocean, of the land called Cape Cod. The geologists have predicted that the entire peninsula will disappear in ten thousand years. There is, however, no need for immediate concern.

The span of years, since the Atlantic coast settlements began in the early 17th century, have seen countless maritime disasters. In 1717, the pirate ship *Whidah* was wrecked on April 26 during a gale. The vessel struck the outer bars at Wellfleet and broke up, spilling her 146 man crew into the water. Only two men were reported to have survived the wreck. During the subsequent events that followed, Massachusetts Governor Shute sent Captain Cyprian Southack to Wellfleet with orders to recover the goods from the ship but the local wreckers had picked her bones clean. He reported that most of the cargo of the *Whidah* had disappeared. The local residents seemed to know nothing about it and tended to ignore the demands of the authorities. It is well documented that there were many people on the beach following the shipwreck. It is also a popular belief that most of the loot was recovered. Even if a heavy surf had prevailed, the knowledge that gold might have been aboard the ship would be a further incentive for those on the beach to take added risks for greater rewards. A pirate treasure may have fallen into welcome hands on the outer Cape. In the early days, it seemed that every storm caused one or more wrecks on the shore. These were usually merchant ships coming in from overseas or a coastal trader with a run of bad luck. The salvage of these ships or their cargoes was part of the economy on eighteenth century Cape Cod.

Local travel to and from the cities was carried out either by stagecoach or packet boats. The packets began somewhere around 1800. One story, handed down from one generation to another, relates that a farmer in Eastham wanted to carry his onions to the market in Boston. He engaged a fishing vessel for this purpose. He decided to go along and oversee the sale. Soon, another friend joined him for the trip. When a neighbor wanted to know why the farmer was leaving on a fishing vessel, the word passed around and quickly, the Captain had other passengers with business in the city. It didn't take long for the idea to catch on and the business of carrying freight and passengers became more lucrative than fishing. In the middle part of the 19th century, packet vessels were carrying full loads of cargo to and from the city from almost every town on Cape Cod. The towns with regular service were: Sandwich, Falmouth, Barnstable, Yarmouth, Dennis and East Dennis. Others were Chatham, Orleans, Eastham, Wellfleet, Truro and Provincetown. Service improved and passengers were accommodated in comfortable cabins. Meals were served to seasoned travelers while the first timers usually hugged the rails until they got their sea legs.

Above: The popular illustrated magazine Harpers Weekly provided some vivid drawings of marine disasters along the coastline. The title of this art was "Winter on the Atlantic. - A United States Revenue Cutter assisting a ship in distress." *Drawing by J.O.Davidson.* **Below:** A very fine line illustration of the seven man crew of a Massachusetts Humane Society boat going to the aid of a stricken vessel caught on the bar off Highland Light in North Truro. Many of these early illustrations were almost life-like. *Photo from the collection of Richard M. Boonisar, Norwell, Mass.*

The packets carried a varying list of passengers. The deep water Captain used the vessels to return home to the Cape after a long voyage. Often his wife would travel to the city to meet her husband and they would come home together. When conditions were right, the Captains of the packets would race each other on the run to the city. The ships carried romantic names such as *Winged Hunter, Eagle Flight* and *Emerald.*

The packets were most always the same type of vessel, the two masted schooner of one hundred tons or less. The journey to Boston by stagecoach was sometimes a lesson in futility. Bad roads and the fording of streams tended to dissuade even the most hardy traveler. The Packet boats, however, usually were the most reliable. It was only a one or two day trip depending on the weather and wind direction. The Packets did a good business until 1848 when the first rail lines to Cape Cod were laid down and by 1870, regular train schedules were maintained. The change was gradual however and a few Packets were still carrying freight into the early 1900's. Communication by telegraph was established between Cape Cod and Boston in 1855 but telephone service was not installed until 1882.

There were some peculiar maritime disasters that occurred off Cape Cod. In March, 1849, the ship ***Franklin*** struck near Newcomb's Hollow on the backside at Wellfleet. It was a rare case of barratry. The owners had conspired to wreck the ship and collect the insurance. But the plot failed when the Captain and other members of the crew were lost while trying to launch a boat from the grounded vessel. Evidence of wrong doing was found in the Captain's papers when they washed ashore on the beach. Part of her cargo was seedlings of trees - lindens, pear, apple, plum and other fruit. The cuttings from these plants still grow in Wellfleet today.

In April of 1849, another tragic loss occurred off Truro when the British ship *Josephus* was wrecked with the loss of twenty-five men. The vessel grounded on the outer bar in fog. When the sea came up, the full rigged ship was pounded by huge waves. The heavy seas brought her masts down and members of her crew clung to small portions of the wreck still above water. Two men launched a boat from shore only to be lost when they were swept under by a big wave. After nightfall, the lightkeeper from Highland light trekked down the beach and found one survivor still alive. He was brought to the lighthouse and ultimately recovered from his ordeal.

Another maritime disaster occurred in 1772, when the schooner *Thomas Nickerson* was discovered off shore flying a distress signal. When it was boarded, one crewman was found alive along with the bodies of three murdered men. The vessel had left Boston, bound for Chatham with a crew of four and a boy. The surviving crewman told of pirates boarding the schooner, killing the crewmen and carrying off the boy. He further claimed that he had hidden below while the crimes had been committed. A search for the pirates was unsuccessful and there were doubts to the story. The man was charged and tried twice, but was acquitted both times for lack of evidence. The victims were all from Chatham. They were Captain Thomas Nickerson, Elisha Newcomb and William Kent, Jr.

There are several danger areas along the Cape shoreline where ships were frequently wrecked. Peaked Hill Bars off Provincetown and Chatham Bars took the highest toll but other locations along the forty mile stretch of beach were the scenes of some spectacular wrecks. Race Point, Highland Light, Nauset Beach and Monomoy Island all had their share of disasters.

These deplorable conditions for mariners did not go unnoticed. In the year 1786, the Massachusetts Humane Society was established to relieve the sufferings of the sailor cast ashore. Small closed sheds were erected along the outer coastline and stocked with canned foods, firewood and first aid kits. The odds were not all that good for the sailor. He first had to survive the shipwreck. Following that, he would have to find his way to the Humane House and hope that vandals had not consumed the food and burned up the firewood inside. The situation was not ideal but it was better than nothing. In addition to the small huts, the Humane Society erected buildings to house surfboats. These were manned by volunteers who went to the aid of sailors in distress when their vessels grounded off shore. The usual event of shipwreck occurred during some of the worst northeast storms and aid was rarely forthcoming. For anyone to be out on the beach in a raging storm was rare indeed. The dangers of launching a boat from the beach in heavy surf conditions were great but there were times when the volunteers carried out some important rescues.

Above: One of the very early stations of the U.S. Life Saving Service at Cahoon's Hollow in Wellfleet on the outer Cape. Of the seven men in the photo, five are identified. D. Haley, F. Atwood, J. Kemp, N. Hayman and D. Cole-Keeper. *Photo courtesy of Richard M. Boonisar.* **Below:** This is a line drawing of one original 1874 United States Life-Saving stations with ornate trim and outside buttresses. The center part of the roof supported a lookout platform. This fixture remained until 1882 when it was enclosed to protect the men from cold weather. Some of these beautiful buildings still stand today.

In 1802, a report to the Trustees of the Humane Society contained a description of the outer beach of Cape Cod. The article identified the locations of the six huts along the coast, which had been erected by the Trustees, "Where shipwrecked seamen may look for shelter." They authorized the printing of 2,000 copies of the report to be distributed among the Custom-houses and insurance offices in the Commonwealth. From those sources, further distribution to coastal shipping was carried out. The huts were located in Provincetown, Eastham, Orleans and Chatham. Locations of the four southern huts have long since been eroded away by the sea. A description given of the huts was as follows: "The six huts were of all one size and shape. Each hut stands on piles, it is eight feet long, eight feet wide, and eight feet high; a sliding door is on the south, a sliding shutter on the west, and a pole, rising fifteen feet above the top of the building, on the east. Within, it is supplied with either straw or hay; and is further accommodated with a bench." The huts were truly not designed for comfort by today's standards but, Spartan as they were, they afforded a cold and wet shipwreck survivor some relief. The report recommended that additional huts be constructed in six other locations along the dangerous shoreline to aid the shipwrecked mariner.

In 1790, Alexander Hamilton, the first Secretary of the Treasury asked Congress to create the Revenue Cutter Service to help collect the tariffs on commerce for support of the United States and to help pay off its debts. Congress, after the usual squabbles, authorized the construction of ten cutters and the men to sail them. The patrols along the Atlantic coastline proved efficient and while entering or leaving port the Captains gathered navigational information about the rivers, inlets, bays and coasts to aid commercial vessels. The United States Coast Guard still carries out this same duty today. The Revenue Cutters were successful and the country paid off its debts in only six years. Later, in 1831, winter cruises were ordered for the cutters to aid mariners at sea during the stormy months of the year.

Unfortunately, Cape Cod is truly one of the "graveyards of the Atlantic." The statistics, recorded since the early 1600's reveal an incredible toll of human life and property. The "Report of Ship Canal", published in 1864, was the result of a study by a Joint Committee of the Massachusetts Legislature appointed in 1860. The purpose was to determine the need for a canal between Buzzards Bay and Cape Cod Bay. The committee stated that in the 17 years studied, previous to 1860, the number of maritime disasters was 827. Four steamers, forty ships, seventy-one barks, one- hundred-ninety-one brigs, four-hundred-ninety-two schooners and twenty-nine sloops. They classified the losses as total: 500, partial: 327. The committee added that the figures were conservative and probably below the actual number. This would average about thirty total wrecks per year. The report added that the greatest number of wrecks occurred during the winter months of November, December and January. The total dollar value of the losses was estimated at about ten million dollars. The loss of human life was estimated to be at about twenty persons per year in all of the wrecks, total and partial. The summary of the report stated that it would be of tremendous advantage to build the canal, both in the saving of life and property. However, construction was not to begin until June 22, 1909. In the 45 intervening years, another nine-hundred wrecks were recorded around Cape Cod and the offshore islands of Martha's Vineyard and Nantucket.

In 1871, the act improving the Life Saving stations along the nation's coastlines was passed by the U.S. Congress and additional stations were erected on Cape Cod. The annual report for the fiscal year ending June 30, 1878 listed fourteen stations on the coast of Massachusetts. Nine of these were on the Cape situated between Race Point in Provincetown and Monomoy Island in Chatham. The report meticulously detailed each of the rescues performed by the Government men along the shore. Under the disasters where there were fatalities, the report described three separate shipwrecks on the same day in which eighteen men lost their lives. On January 3, 1878, the American schooner *J.G.Babcock* was wrecked in Orleans with the loss of seven men. Further to the north, the schooners *Addie P. Avery* and *Pow-wow* came ashore in Truro with the loss of eleven men. The establishment of the U.S. Life Saving Service on Cape Cod brought a surprising decline in the carnage along the shoreline. Records reveal that in sixteen years, from 1873 to 1889, from vessels and cargoes valued at seven million dollars, less than two million dollars was posted in losses. From a total of 3,259 persons aboard these vessels, only 52 lost their lives. This was a significant change in shipping losses as compared to the previous report by the canal committee, where in seventeen years, 1843 to 1859, a ten million dollar loss in property was reported and over three hundred fatalities.

Above: On the stormy night of December 26, 1872, the Hamburg barque *Frances* was wrecked on the beach at Truro, Massachusetts, one mile from the Highland Lighthouse. The vessel was badly iced up, as there was a northeast gale blowing at the time of the wreck. Cape Cod Life Savers rescued the crew of 14 by surf boat. *Photo courtesy of Mystic Seaport, Mystic Conn.* **Below:** In the mid 1930's Admiral Donald MacMillan of Provincetown, made some photographs of the *Frances* wreck from the beach. The photo is a close up of the bow section. Wreckage of the iron hull vessel is still visible today at Head of the Meadow Beach in Truro. *Photo from the collection of Clive Driver, Provincetown, Mass.*

The value of the breeches buoy apparatus is evident in this illustration where the men of the ship climbed into the rigging of a sunken vessel and lashed the hawser to the top of the broken mast. Two people could be carried in the breeches buoy without strain on the gear.

The dangers of navigation around Cape Cod were evident. Prudent shipmasters with a keen weather eye practiced caution and were successful in the coastal trades. Those Captains with years of experience around the shoal waters of southeastern New England passed their knowledge of local conditions down to their sons but even the best navigators, caught on a lee shore during a northeaster, will ultimately end up wrecked on the beach. The exact number of ships and men lost around Cape Cod and the offshore islands will never be known. It is likely that the figures would approach thousands of both, ships and men. Early wreck reports were sometimes written as small notices in annual town reports. Many were probably never recorded. Hundreds of ships sailed and went missing. No one knows how many of these might have been wrecked and sunk just off shore.

Stormy weather is the primary cause of shipwrecks along the shores of Cape Cod. In the 19th century there were no advance forecasts to warn the mariner of approaching storms. Many vessels leaving port in good weather were never heard from again. Storms are mixtures of air masses. The natural sequence in the birth of a storm occurs when a pool of warm air moves up from the southern Atlantic and collides with cool air from the north. A severe cyclonic storm develops just off the coast. As it moves northward, winds increase around the center and reach velocities of 50 to 60 miles per hour. When the low pressure area moves toward New England it frequently turns northeast as it approaches Long Island and heads out over the waters of the north Atlantic. The center of the storm occasionally will pass over Cape Cod but more often it goes to the east creating rough seas and high winds along the backside.

Left: In a Nantucket cemetary stands the gravestone of Robert Ratliff. The inscription carries his life history: *"Born at New Castle upon the Tyne, England on Feb. 25, 1794 - Died at Nantucket Feb. 20, 1882, age 88. He was a seaman on board the ship Northumberland, 84 guns, under command of Sir George Cockburn that conveyed Napoleon Buonaparte to St. Helena in 1815 and received marked notice from the great emperor. He was also a seaman in the Albion, 74, in the attack on the city of Washington in 1814.*
"In 1820, he was shipwrecked on the island of Nantucket where he resided the remainder of his life. He was well known as a successful master rigger for fifty years. Honored for his integrity, respected for his uniform courtesy and beloved for his kindness and generosity." Photograph by the Author. **Below:** Several photographs have turned up around Cape Cod of wreckage on the beach which is unidentified. This one is from the collection of Joseph A, Nickerson of Chatham. Written on the back of the photograph is: *"Wreck - North Beach" - A list of names follows: " Miss Mabel Nickerson; Miss Marie L. Freeman; Mr. Tom Nickerson and Mr. Edward Houghton. Taken by W.H. Weed."*

At the present time, weather records date back a hundred years or more. Some early information can been found in the history of the Plymouth Colony. The August 1635 storm was described as a severe tempest causing wrecks and disasters all along the shore. Almost a century later, in 1713, another gale hit the New England coast and heavy damage occurred along the Cape Cod shores with high tides and waves. More storms were recorded in 1786, 1804, 1815, and the triple storms of December, 1839. The 1839 storms inspired Henry Wadsworth Longfellow to write his classic shipwreck poem "The Wreck of the Hesperus." One of the most tragic storms off Cape Cod occurred on October 3, 1841. Fifty-seven men were lost from the town of Truro when seven vessels foundered in the gale. More were lost from other towns; ten from Yarmouth and twenty from Dennis. The men were fishing on Georges Bank when the storm hit. They set sail and headed for Cape Cod but never reached port because of the severe conditions. The gale of 1851 was notable as the "Minot's Light Storm," when the lighthouse on the Cohasset Ledge was toppled by huge waves. Another great storm in 1853 pushed over the piers on the bayside and a schooner was tossed up on Sandy Neck. All hands were drowned. Another wild storm in December of 1873 wrecked two large ships on the outer Cape. The ship *Peruvian* went down on Peaked Hill Bars and the bark *Frances* was wrecked on the outer bar in Truro. Weather on Cape Cod varies with the season. In the summer, prevailing winds are west and southwest. Variable northwest and west winds generally indicate fair weather as do north and northeast winds with a high barometer. In the springtime dense fogs are prevalent over Nantucket and Vineyard sounds. When gentle southwest winds blow, the fog spreads over the entire Cape. This phenomenon is due to the warm winds from the south blowing over the cool water surrounding the Cape and low clouds form near the surface. When the surrounding waters warm up in late June the foggy periods diminish. The peninsula is subject to different types of storms throughout the year but the most destructive storm is a hurricane.

Hurricanes are born in the Atlantic, often somewhere north of the equator off the coast of Dakar in Africa. The prevailing winds move the storm in a westerly direction. Occasionally, the hurricane is influenced by a Bermuda high pressure area and it may take a turn to the north. The whirling clouds and winds move along the coast and then turn northeasterly. They may change direction any time without warning. They are dangerous and unpredictable. The storm follows a course over warm water which provides much of the heat to fuel the action. When it reaches the cooler waters of the North Atlantic, the storm slows down and usually dissipates. One of the most famous hurricanes in modern history was the Portland Gale of November 26 and 27, 1898. The blizzard raged at full intensity for thirty-six hours with seventy mile per hour winds. The wind whipped waters cast ships ashore like driftwood and many vessels were lost on the backside of Cape Cod. Thirty-six were lost in Provincetown harbor. Scores of sailing vessels were wrecked in Vineyard Haven harbor where they had sought shelter from the storm. There was a total of one hundred and forty ships sunk or wrecked. The most notable was the passenger steamer *Portland* with all hands, between 170 and 200 persons were aboard the ship when she sank a few miles northeast of Provincetown. Another famous hurricane occurred in September of 1938. The storm hit the state of Rhode Island the hardest killing over 600 persons and causing over three hundred million dollars in property damage. The entire waterfront area of the state; docks, piers, yachts and cottages were devastated. It was weeks before normal services were resumed.

Above: The crew of a Cape Cod life-saving station are pictured as they haul out the beach cart. This was an efficiency drill staged once a week. The men are in white warm weather uniforms. **Below:** This illustration depicts the life-savers hauling the breeches buoy apparatus to the scene of a wreck. The men hauling the cart through the surf wash showed the ultimate need for horse power that was later used in rescue work.

These two illustrations were taken from the U.S. Life Saving Service Beach-Apparatus Drill handbook. The drawing above depicts the relative positions of the men while setting up the lines for the drill. The drawing below shows the complete set-up of the apparatus with the men in proper positions to bring a survivor ashore. The apparatus was simple and easy to use. This method of rescue was used for a hundred years until modern technology retired the breeches buoy. Today, helicopters perform this duty without the survivors getting even their feet wet.

THE TRURO DISASTER

The dried salt codfish industry had been a mainstay of the New England economy since the very early days. This began to change in the middle of the 19th century when the market for fresh fish started to develop. The ports closest to the fresh fish at Georges Bank were on Cape Cod. The Cape Codders took advantage of the proximity of the resource but the winter storms took a toll on the vessels. Seventy-eight men were lost in an 1837 storm. But by far the greatest tragedy occurred when a late fall gale swept up the east coast on October 2, 1841 and decimated the fishing fleet on Georges Bank. The hardest hit town on Cape Cod was Truro which lost seven fishing vessels and fifty-seven sailors. Most of the men were young but the disaster left nineteen widows and thirty-nine children without fathers. The town went into mourning and a fund was set up to aid the families of the men lost in the tragedy. One other town, Dennis, lost twenty-two of her men in the same storm. The total for all of Cape Cod was fourteen vessels and 87 men. The storm raged for four days before it abated. There were several wrecks along the back shore in addition to the ones off shore.

The noted disaster of October 2, 1841 is remembered in Truro at the old burial ground. A marble shaft was erected with the names and ages of the 57 men lost in the terrible storm when seven vessels from that town sank during the tremendous gale. The sides of the monument contain the names and ages of the fifty-seven men lost. The following ephitah was etched on the front of the stone:

SACRED to the memory of 57 citizens of Truro who were lost in seven vessels, which foundered at sea in the memorable gale of Oct. 3, 1841.

Then shall the dust return to the earth as it was; and the spirit shall return to the god who gave it.

Man goeth to his long home and the mourners go about the streets.

One of the victims of the Truro disaster was George E. Anderson. His gravestone marks the resting place of his wife Mehitable. The etching on the stone reads:

GEO. E. ANDERSON

Lost at sea Oct. 3, 1841. Age 30 Yrs. 5 Mos.

MEHITABLE

Wife of George E. Anderson, Died July 24, 1851, Age 40 Yrs. 8 Mos.

The storms in the mid nineteenth century always took a toll on the fishing fleet. In 1841, there were no warnings of approaching storms to alert the fisherman. The boats were a hundred miles at sea when the storm hit, a full days sail from home. At this time, there were two ways to make a living on Cape Cod. Farming or going to sea. There were, however, diversions for these men along the shore when a vessel was wrecked on the beach. Wrecking was a way of life for some and a lucky break for others. The Cape Codders of yesterday were a frugal people who were not wealthy. They had to live by their wits and anything that washed up on shore was "finders keepers". The crops grown, usually fed the family and left a little over to help with expenses, but no one got rich behind a plow. The part time wrecker walked the beaches in search of flotsam and jetsam. The best times were during those stormy nights and days when a ship might come ashore or run aground on the outer bars. These men were paid well when they could help kedge a ship off a reef. When all else failed, and the vessel was a complete wreck, the Cape men aided in salvage of the cargo where possible. This was very profitable and particularly if the crew was lost. With the coming of lighthouses, the accidental wrecks were fewer but the storms and disasters continued. At one time, there was a small community at Monomoy Point. These men made their living by wrecking and salvage. The shoals in this area were dangerous and a constant source of business for the wreckers. Often, the Monomoy men could work a vessel off into deep water by dropping cargo over the side to lighten the vessel. At other times, when a ship could not be saved, they salvaged the cargo and saved the crew. It was, again, no way to get rich, but it was a living.

Above: The aftermath of a shipwreck. These logs strewn along Nauset Beach was the result of a wreck broken on the outer bar, and the cargo washed ashore. The men in the background were probably salvage men. The logs were valuable and were most likely carted off the beach to be sold. *Photo by Bessie Penniman, courtesy of the Cape Cod National Seashore Park.* **Below:** Schooner traffic along the back side of Cape Cod is evident in this photograph taken before the turn of the century. Note on the horizon off shore just to the right of the roof is a four masted schooner. A little further ahead just over the dune is a three master. This photo was taken in the Tonset area of Orleans. *Photo by Henry K. Cummings.*

Chapter Two

The development of this country's technology expanded rapidly in the 19th century. Transportation between trading centers was vital to a flourishing economy. Goods and material moved in coastal trading ships. Lumber, coal, cotton and agricultural products moved north from the southern states and manufactured goods moved south from the northern states. Over 30,000 ships per year rounded Cape Cod. The establishment of the United States Life Saving Service did much to ameliorate the plight of the shipwrecked sailors but the Life Savers were, however, only human. A bad storm with high seas sometimes made rescues impossible. Life Savers often did the incredible. They saved ships and men in situations beyond belief. Occasionally, mistakes were made in some rescue attempts and many servicemen lost their lives. The Life Saving Service issued annual reports to Congress and other marine organizations outlining the operations for the fiscal year. The 1880 report contained some important statistics:

"The number of casualties upon the Atlantic coast within the scope of the service last year was one less than in the previous year, being 162, while on the Great Lakes the number is more than doubled, being 136 against 53 of the year anterior. In these 136 disasters only a single life was lost. The total loss of life within the scope of the service is the smallest ever reached since its general extension, the lowest previous number being 22. Of the 9 persons lost, one was a woman cook left asleep in the cabin of a foundering vessel by the deserting crew, and drowned while the life-boat was on its way to the rescue; two were fishermen, who sank from a capsized yawl before the surf-boat could reach the scene; four were sailors, who perished on a fair night by the swift breaking up of a rotten vessel on stranding; the other two were seamen, who fell through exhaustion from the rigging of a schooner as she dragged her anchors along the coast in the great storm of February 3, followed on the beach by the life-saving crew, with the apparatus, who had to await her coming to a stand to effect line communication."

The general summary for the years 1871 to 1880, covering the entire coastline of the United States, listed 1,097 maritime disasters with a value of the vessels totaling $13,339,073. The net worth of their cargoes was $7,118,662. The value of the property saved was listed at $12,130,215 and the property lost was $8,327,520. The total number of persons on board these vessels was 10,381. The number of persons lost was 371. Of this number, one hundred and eighty-three were lost in two tragic disasters on the North Carolina coast. The report continued with details on the repairs and rebuilding of the old stations. It listed the establishment of new stations. There were also recommendations to improve the service. At this time there were nine stations on Cape Cod and one on the island of Nantucket. They were: Race Point and Peaked Hill Bars in Provincetown, the Highlands and Pamet River stations in Truro, Cahoon's Hollow in Wellfleet and Nauset station in Eastham. Further south, the Orleans, Chatham and Monomoy stations. One station was listed on Nantucket at Surfside, two and one half miles south of the town. In the ensuing years, four more stations were built on Cape Cod. The Wood End station in Provincetown, the High Head in Truro, the Old Harbor in Chatham and the Monomoy Point station at the tip of Monomoy Island in Chatham. Additional stations were also built on the offshore islands. The Coskata and Madaquet on Nantucket, the Muskeget on Muskeget Island, the Gay Head station on Martha's Vineyard and the Cuttyhunk station on the westernmost island in the Elizabeth chain. This made a total of eighteen stations, each with six to nine men, depending on the size of the area covered by that station.

Above: The launch of the surfboat. This illustration was used several times in Harpers Weekly to depict the life-savers on their way to a wreck. **Below:** This illustration from Harpers depicts the self-righting life-boat under sail going to the aid of a wrecked vessel in heavy surf.

Returning from the wreck. An artists touch up of a photograph showing the Life Savers in action along the shore, bringing in a survivor of a shipwreck.

The layout of the Life Saving Stations along the coastline of Cape Cod was designed to enable the coverage of the surfmen to overlap the shore and protect the area. In the daytime, lookouts in towers ranged the entire beach. At night and in thick weather, men patrolled the beach on foot looking for wrecks. If a vessel was spotted near shore the man on patrol burned a Coston signal (flare), to warn the ship off. If a wreck was seen, the same signal was used to notify the sailors on board that help was on the way. Situated between the stations were the half-way houses. When the patrol from the northern station arrived there, he met the man from the station to the south. They exchanged a small brass check with the number of the station stamped on it. When the man completed his patrol, he turned in the check to the keeper to verify that he had completed his beach patrol properly. The Life Savers had other duties beside the walking patrols. The men held a different drill each day of the week to maintain their proficiency. Breeches buoy, surf-boat, sailing and signal practice were taught, re-taught and practiced year round. Life Savers led an odd existence. Long stretches of boredom during watch, were sometimes interrupted by periods of sheer terror while attempting a rescue over towering waves in a small boat during a howling northeaster.

Above: The Life Saving Service issued small waterproof booklets on "Instructions to Mariners in case of Shipwreck." The publication could be carried in a sailor's pocket for quick reference. **Below:** The booklet had illustrations on many pages along with specific data on what to do when shipwrecked.

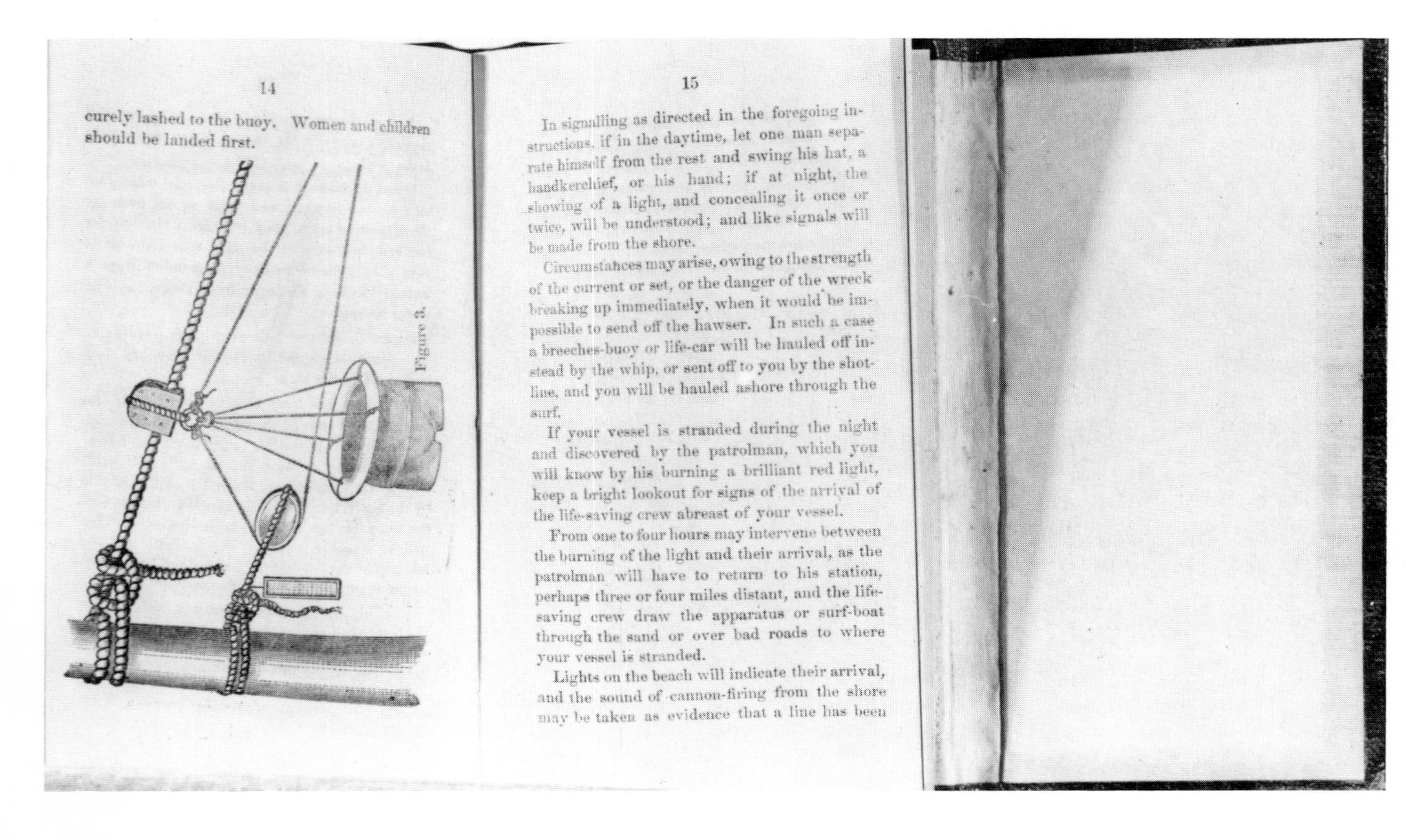

14

curely lashed to the buoy. Women and children should be landed first.

Figure 3.

15

In signalling as directed in the foregoing instructions, if in the daytime, let one man separate himself from the rest and swing his hat, a handkerchief, or his hand; if at night, the showing of a light, and concealing it once or twice, will be understood; and like signals will be made from the shore.

Circumstances may arise, owing to the strength of the current or set, or the danger of the wreck breaking up immediately, when it would be impossible to send off the hawser. In such a case a breeches-buoy or life-car will be hauled off instead by the whip, or sent off to you by the shot-line, and you will be hauled ashore through the surf.

If your vessel is stranded during the night and discovered by the patrolman, which you will know by his burning a brilliant red light, keep a bright lookout for signs of the arrival of the life-saving crew abreast of your vessel.

From one to four hours may intervene between the burning of the light and their arrival, as the patrolman will have to return to his station, perhaps three or four miles distant, and the life-saving crew draw the apparatus or surf-boat through the sand or over bad roads to where your vessel is stranded.

Lights on the beach will indicate their arrival, and the sound of cannon-firing from the shore may be taken as evidence that a line has been

U.S.L.S.S. BOOKLETS

In 1881, the Life Saving Service issued small pocket size booklets with "Instructions to mariners in case of Shipwreck". The small publication contained all the necessary information needed by sailors on board a vessel aground on a lee shore. The second page contained general information in easy to read language to acquaint the mariner with the locations and operations of the Life Saving Service:

"Life-saving stations, life-boat stations, and houses of refuge are located upon the Atlantic and Pacific seaboard of the United States, the Gulf of Mexico, and the Lake coasts, as shown in the list in the latter part of this book, the latitude and longitude being given so far as determined.

"All stations on the Atlantic coast from the eastern extremity of the State of Maine to Cape Fear, North Carolina, are manned annually by crews of experienced surfmen from the 1st of September until the 1st of May following.

"All life-saving and life-boat stations are fully supplied with boats, wreck-gun, beach apparatus, restoratives, & c."

The booklet continued with other general information about houses of refuge in other states. Also, provisions provided for the shipwrecked sailors; instructions in handling life-saving breeches buoy rigging and what to do in case of rescue by surfboat. The book contained diagrams and further instructions. A sailor who studied the book and learned all of the pertinent data would stand a good chance of surviving a shipwreck if he was lucky. The details contained in the booklet required a knowledge of the terms and rescue gear described. The back of the book contained a list of two-hundred Life Saving Stations and houses of refuge which were existing at that time with their locations. The printing in the book was very fine and it was not recommended reading while one was hanging in the rigging of a wrecked vessel with seas breaking over the hull.

The crew of the Life Saving Station. This photograph was taken at the Gurnet Point Life Saving Station. The young men were posing for the photographer with their uniforms which consisted of hats and jackets.

Above: This unidentified photograph is from the collection of Bessie Pennimen in the Cape Cod National Seashore. Thousands of hulls ended up on the Cape shores for any kind of salvage the Cape Codders could pick from them. There is a man aboard, probably for the purpose of cutting out firewood. **Below:** An unidentified three masted schooner on the beach. The photograph was taken just after the vessel came ashore as the sails have not yet been salvaged. The hull in this position is most usually a total loss with the surf breaking over the hull and spray flying in the air.

The U.S. Life Saving Service performed their duties along both coasts and in the Great Lakes. The Cape Cod Lifesavers were a unique group with an area unlike any other in the country. The stations were situated about three to five miles apart and placed in the sand dunes, well above the high water mark. The men employed as Lifesavers were all skilled Cape Cod boatmen. Coastal watermen, packet sailors and fishermen had the experience needed to fulfill the requirements. These men were imbued with the traditions of their predecessors. Drills and discipline helped to develop the character of the surfmen. Devotion to duty and steadfast integrity completed the picture of the Cape Cod Lifesaver. These qualities were needed and often put to the test while carrying out their normal duties. The dangers of a routine night patrol were often manifold. A six mile walk on a wind swept beach with sharp particles of sand cutting exposed areas of the skin; storm tossed tides flooding low beaches and creating areas of quicksand, cutting the man off from his station; hours and even days of heavy labor on the beach or pulling a boat without relief, made the Cape Cod Lifesaver a cut above the rest. These men, working with long experience in attending wrecked ships and saving imperiled crews, were extraordinary. The frequency of disasters around Cape Cod and the Islands required the best men the service could procure. While most Cape Cod boatmen qualified to be surfmen, some of those hired did not share the same enthusiasm for the occupation as the majority of the Lifesavers. They maintained a low profile for the financial security that a Government job presented even though there were no retirement benefits in the Life Saving Service. Frequently, however, when faced with a dangerous mission, the man without courage was left on the beach and dismissed from the service.

The Life Saving Station was a large spacious building of one and a half stories, between 18 and 20 feet wide and 40 to 45 feet long. On the ground floor the boatroom occupied almost two thirds of the floor space. The second floor was used as sleeping quarters for the crew. The active season for all stations with few exceptions began on August 30th each year and continued through June 30th of the following year. During the months of July and August the stations were unmanned except for the Keeper. Most stations were equipped with two lifeboats and two sets of breeches buoy apparatus along with life preservers, coston signals, rockets, patrol lanterns, signal flags, medicine chests, comfortable furniture and a lookout tower on top to maintain a watch over the surrounding beach area. All stations on Cape Cod were connected by telephones. After 1880, horses were employed at most stations to aid the surfmen in pulling the equipment to the scene of a wreck. The beach cart with the breeches buoy apparatus weighed almost one thousand pounds and was a difficult pull for six men through snow drifts or soft beach sand. The lifeboat cart was equally heavy, requiring strong exertions of labor to move. Life at the station consisted of standing watches and attending to the routine of the day. On Mondays, the men cleaned the station and put it in order. Tuesday was reserved for the lifeboat drills. On Wednesday, the men studied and practiced the international code of signals with flags. The breeches buoy drill was conducted on Thursday. On Fridays they instructed the men in the art of resuscitation of drowned persons. Saturday was wash day and Sunday morning was devoted to religious services.

The tragic loss of the Keeper and two surfmen of the Peaked Hill Bars Life Saving Station was recorded in 1880. At 4 a.m. on November 30, the sloop *C.E. Trumbull* of Rockport, Massachusetts with a crew of 6 men stranded on the outer bar near the Peaked Hill station in Provincetown. The vessel was bound from New Bedford for her home port with a cargo of 20 tons of coal when she grounded 400 yards from shore. Surfman Charles P. Kelley discovered the ship as be was beginning his patrol. He burned a coston signal to inform the sloop's crew that help was on the way. The weather was clear and the surf was low near the shore but out on the bar the sea was running high.

Keeper David H. Atkins ordered the surf-boat launched. The boat was manned by surfmen Stephen F. Mayo, Elisha M. Taylor, Isaiah Young, Charles P. Kelley and Samuel O. Fisher with Keeper Atkins on the steering oar. The sixth surfman at the station John L. Cole was ordered to stand on shore and keep the lanterns burning to guide the boat back to shore. The first trip to the grounded sloop successfully brought four of her crewmen ashore. When the lifesavers returned for the other two men, Keeper Atkins shouted for them to cut the main sheet and let go the boom. A sloop with her mast set far forward has a boom, eighty to ninety feet long. The mainsail aboard the *Trumbull* was double reefed with the sail full and the end of the boom dipping in and out of the water as the vessel rolled in the rough seas. The two men ignored the order from Keeper Atkins.

As the surfboat approached, the sloop rolled over. The boom went underwater, snagged the side of the boat and flipped it over spilling the lifesaving crew into the sea.

The Lifesavers had to try and save themselves. They were cold and wet while battling huge waves. The boat was righted but only to be overturned again by the heavy surf. Surfmen Young, Kelley and Fisher managed to struggle ashore and were assisted by surfman Cole who was unaware of the disaster until the survivors washed ashore in their cork life jackets. The sloop

This is an artist's conception of the conditions at Peaked Hill Bars on the morning of November 30, 1880. The crew of the Life Saving station was tossed into the water by the mainsail boom of the sloop *C.E. Trumbull* of Rockport, Massachusetts. Three men were lost in the accident. *Drawing by Paul C. Morris, Nantucket, Mass.*

worked off the outer bar and drifted down the backside of the Cape. It was boarded off Chatham by wreckers who repaired her sails and took her to Boston. The bodies of Keeper Atkins; surfmen Taylor and Mayo washed ashore later in the morning. Funeral services were conducted in Provincetown a few days later. Surfman Young was crippled for life from the ordeal. Surfmen Kelley and Fisher returned to duty.

This loss of these men on Cape Cod usually served as a reminder to the Life Savers to maintain vigilance in their duty. By contrast, the 1883 annual report related a successful rescue by the men of the Orleans Station. "Good service was rendered on the stormy morning of January 10, 1883 by the crew of the men of this station on the wreck of the bark *Friedericke* of Stettin, Germany." A heavy northeast gale was blowing at the time with thick snow falling. Huge seas were breaking on the beach when the bark, out of Pillau, Prussia, for Portland Maine, struck the outer bar one quarter mile south of the station. The accident occurred in the late morning and was immediately seen by a surfman at the station who sounded the alarm. Keeper Marcus M. Pierce and his crew quickly went into action. They hauled out the mortar cart and started for the wreck. The going was difficult in snow drifts and the men labored for an hour before arriving at the scene. When the gun was fired, the line laid across the end of the foreyard and jib-boom. The whip line was sent off and then the hawser. The crew of eleven men was brought ashore in less than thirty minutes. They were taken to the station for dry clothes and hot food. The vessel proved a total loss but her cargo of rags was salvaged. The crew of the bark remained at the station for three days.

Sometimes the rescue efforts of the Life-savers ended in frustration. On March 15, 1887, the schooner *J.H. Eels* stranded on the outer bar about a mile and a half south of the Nauset station in Eastham during a northeast snowstorm. The Life-savers under Keeper Knowles immediately launched a surfboat to rescue the crew of the schooner who were holding on to the jib- boom. The heavy sea sweeping in over the bar made it impossible to approach the vessel, even near enough to throw a line. The swift current carried the boat away from the ship and the surf crashed over the Life-savers nearly swamping their boat several times. The effort was futile and Keeper Knowles ordered the boat ashore and sent four men to the station for the breeches buoy apparatus. The Lyle gun was set up and a shot line fired out to the schooner. The first one fell short of the wreck by about forty yards. When the second shot was fired the line broke. The third fell short again and the line parted on the fourth and fifth shots. The Keeper sent men back to the station for more line and the tide was rising, pushing the men back to the top of the dunes.

At this time, another gun was pressed into service. The Hunt gun from the Mass. Humane Society station was charged and fired. The shot fell about 75 yards short of the wreck. Another shot fell short. The Keeper then charged the gun with extra powder. The final shot soared out over the wreck. It fell between the fore and main masts about twenty feet above the men on the wreck. Two of the men clambered up into the rigging and hauled in the line. The Life-savers sent out the whip line slowly but the strong current pulled the line so far to the south that it could not be landed aboard the schooner. With only two men to haul the line out, the current was stronger than they could overcome. The whole operation was tried again with the Life-savers carrying the line two hundred yards to the north before sending it off shore but the debilitated condition of the two men on the wreck reduced the chances of success. By this time it was growing too dark to continue operations. After dark, a watch was set up on the beach and at daylight another attempt was made to launch the surfboat but the seas were running higher than the day before so the idea was abandoned. Three men remained on the mast but one was apparently dead. The fourth man had been washed overboard during the night and was lost.

While attempting to launch the surf-boat, a tug was seen coming from the north. The Life-savers signaled from the top of the dunes and the tug came in near the schooner and launched a small boat. After much difficulty they succeeded in removing the two crewmen from the rigging and they were taken aboard the tug. The body of the man washed off the jib-boom was never found. Two days later, the surf subsided enough for the Life-savers to launch a surf-boat and cut down the body from the rigging. The annual report listed the *J.H. Eels* as a two masted schooner of 144 tons out of Camden, Maine. Her master was Fred Wallace. Captain Wallace was one of those lost. She was bound from Perth Amboy, New Jersey to Boston with a cargo of railroad iron. The estimated amount of loss for both vessel and cargo was $17,000.

Above: On the night of December 22, 1884, the Boston schooner *Warren Sawyer* came ashore at Surfside on Nantucket Island around eleven p.m. The crew climbed into the mizzen rigging. The Life Savers fired a shot line over the vessel and set up the breeches buoy. They brought the crew of eight men ashore safely. The ship was laden with cotton and scrap iron. **Below:** Most of her cargo was landed before a January storm broke the ship up. *Photo from the collection of Paul C. Morris, Nantucket, Massachusetts.*

Late in the evening of August 22, 1884, the *U.S.S. Tallapoosa*, a sidewheel Navy steamer, was rammed and sunk in Vineyard Sound by the coal laden schooner *James S. Lowell* of Bath, Maine. The accident occurred on a clear night, and witnesses claimed that both vessels saw the lights of the other. The *Lowell* and other vessels picked up the survivors from the steamer, which went down in ten minutes. Three of the crew of the Naval vessel were lost. The ship was raised and repaired in the New York Naval Shipyard. *Photo by Baldwin Coolidge, courtesy of the Society for the Preservation of New England Antiquities, Boston, Mass.*

Author Henry C. Kitteredge said: "If all the wrecks which have been piled up on the backside of Cape Cod were placed bow to stern, they would make a continuous wall from Chatham to Provincetown." Fortunately, this "wall" never piled up. The numerous accidents supported such a hypothesis but the large number of shipwrecks occurred over a period of three hundred years. The derelict wooden hulls were subject to various forces by the action of the waves. Most of them were covered by sand near the low tide mark. Initially, old and weak hulls were badly shattered or broken by the huge waves that accompany a storm. A newer ship with a strong hull many times could withstand this action and sand later covered the derelict. Periodically, old wrecks are uncovered after a severe storm and usually are covered again by subsequent tides. The other forces involved actions by men. Wooden ships were built of the best timber available and when the ship was wrecked, this material could be salvaged. And, it was free. The only cost was the labor of hauling it off the beach. Cape Cod was stripped of her hardwood forests, as seen by the Pilgrims in 1620, and firewood was at a premium. Much of the wood salvaged from shipwrecks was burned for home heating but some of it was used for building. The design of some early Cape Cod cottages was said to have been influenced by material salvaged from wrecks. Most wood used in ship construction is curved. When salvaging lumber from a wreck, the Cape Codder reportedly framed the roof of his house with these arched timbers. The only beams suitable for this use would be the deck timbers with a slight arch. The outside hull frames of a ship had too sharp a bend to be useful in house construction. Today, one can spot several houses on Cape Cod with bowed roofs, some of which may trace their origin to an early Cape Cod shipwreck. In keeping with some of the old traditions, builders today occasionally build in a new house with a bowed roof.

Above: The schooner *Grecian,* bound from Calais, Maine to New York City with a cargo of coal was wrecked off Chatham on December 6, 1885. The crew of five men were rescued in a lifeboat by volunteers of the Massachusetts Humane Society from Chatham. The schooner was a total loss. *Photo from the collection of Joseph A. Nickerson, Chatham, Mass.* **Below:** The three masted schooner *T. B. Witherspoon* came ashore on the south side of the Island of Nantucket on January 10, 1886, during a blinding snow storm. The crew aboard the vessel had seen the Sankaty Lighthouse and believed it to be Montauk Point Light at the end of Long Island, New York. The miscalculation had laid the vessel ashore. Surf conditions prevented life savers from launching a boat from shore and the crew dropped off, one by one, until of nine aboard, only two persons survived. The schooner was bound from Surinam to Boston with a mixed cargo and she ultimately broke up in the heavy surf. *From an original sketch by John J. Gardner, courtesy of Charles F. Sayle, Nantucket, Mass.*

Above: The American bark *Carrie Wyman* went ashore at Herring Cove in Provincetown on the night of February 4, 1886. The vessel was bound from Turks Island for Boston with a cargo of 18,000 bushels of salt. The ship was trying to make Provincetown Harbor to ride out a storm. The bark was covered with ice and the crew was suffering from frost bite when the grounding occurred. Part of her cargo was unloaded and the vessel was refloated on the night of February 7th. The *Carrie Wyman* was of 459 tons and her home port was in Searsport, Maine. *Photo from the collection of Clive Driver, Provincetown, Mass.* **Below:** The brigantine *Emily T. Sheldon* grounded on the eastern end of Peaked Hill Bars in Provincetown at two o'clock in the afternoon on March 22, 1886. The vessel was seen cruising around Cape Cod for a few days in foggy weather. Her rudder became fouled and she lost steerage. Life Savers launched a boat through heavy surf and saved the crew of eight men. The brigantine was bound from Boothbay, Maine to Annapolis with a load of ice. She dragged up on the beach and became a total loss. *Photo by William Smith, Provincetown, Mass.*

The first set of lighthouses in Chatham was erected in 1808. The towers, made of wood, were 43 feet high and overlooked the Atlantic Ocean. The second set of lighthouses (above) made of brick were built in 1840. *Photo courtesy of the National Archives.* In November 1879 the surf undermined the banking and the brick south tower of the 1840 lighthouse went over the bank. Fifteen months later the north tower fell and there is no evidence of the towers today. A third set of lights (below) was built in Chatham in 1877. *Photo courtesy of Noel Beyle, Eastham, Mass.*

Chapter Three

The United States Lighthouse Service was created by Congress in 1789 to mark the hazardous coastal areas where maritime disasters frequently occurred. The aids to navigation included fog signals, day beacons, buoys and lighthouses. Lightships in American waters came on the scene much later. In 1797, the town of Truro deeded ten acres of the highlands on the ocean front to the Federal Government. The cliffs were 142 feet above sea level and the Highland Light station was established. The lighthouse was 53 feet high and at night could be seen twenty miles off shore. Ultimately there were twenty-eight lighthouse stations around Cape Cod and the offshore islands of Martha's Vineyard and Nantucket. The men of the lighthouse service did their job well until 1939 when the organization was consolidated with the U.S. Coast Guard. The slow but steady spread of automation has retired most all of today's lighthouse keepers. All of the lightships have been retired, replaced by large navigational buoys.

Lighthouses are conspicuous along the Cape Cod shorelines and are among the most picturesque areas frequented by artists and photographers. The history of maritime beacons dates back to 300 B.C. when the Egyptians built a massive tower at the entrance to the port of Alexandria. It was a huge marble building, four-hundred and fifty feet high and had a large bonfire burning on top. At night, the flames assisted mariners finding their way into port. The earliest lighthouse on the Atlantic coast was built on Little Brewster Island in Boston Harbor. It was initially lighted on September 14, 1716. The first Keeper was George Worthylake. He was paid a salary of fifty pounds per year. In 1776, the light was destroyed by British forces evacuating Boston under fire. The Massachusetts Legislature voted to expend 1,450 pounds to erect a new lighthouse. That light still stands today. Congress enacted new laws to create the U.S. Lighthouse Service in 1789 to "support, maintain and repair the lighthouses, fog signals, beacons and buoys on the bays, inlets and harbors of the United States for the purpose of assisting the navigation and safety of maritime traffic." Heretofore the individual coastal states maintained the navigational aids and there were no standards set or practiced. Consequently the upkeep was inadequate for safety. Later, many new lighthouses were built by the Lighthouse Service. They were erected with stones, cast iron and bricks. The structures were built with various designs to blend with the local landscape and for easy identification. Many of the beautiful lighthouses built in the 19th century are historic landmarks today.

From the twenty-eight lighthouse stations, originally located along the shores of Cape Cod and the Islands, eighteen are still in operation today. Beginning in Cape Cod Bay, the Sandy Neck lighthouse at the entrance to Barnstable harbor is no longer operational but the tower still stands. In the bay off Wellfleet, Billingsgate light was located on an island which washed away in the early 1900's. Only a trace of the foundation remains and can be seen at low tide. Mayo's Beach light was situated at the head of the bay in Wellfleet but the station was discontinued around 1900. The light is no longer there but the foundation is still visible. Long Point, Wood End and Race Point lighthouses in Provincetown are still in operation as is the Highland, or Cape Cod light in the town of Truro. Nauset light in Eastham and Chatham light still flash their beacons out to sea every night. Monomoy and Stage Harbor lights in Chatham are no longer in service but their towers are still visible. The Bass River, Point Gamon and Hyannis lights were retired many years ago. A light in Nantucket Sound named Bishops and Clerks, located south of Hyannis, fell into the sea before 1940. Wings Neck lighthouse in Cataumet is no longer operational but the Nobska Point light in the Woods Hole section of Falmouth is still in service as is the newest station on the Cape in Buzzards Bay. The Cleveland Ledge Light was built in 1941 and is situated in the middle of the shipping channel. There have been several near collisions in foggy and thick weather at this station. At the western entrance to Buzzards Bay is a light tower. A red square superstructure on four piles with the word "BUZZARDS" on each side. This structure replaced a lightship at that location in 1961.

On the island of Martha's Vineyard, the East Chop and West Chop lights and Gay Head light are still in service as is the beautiful Edgartown lighthouse at the entrance to the harbor. Recently, on Chappaquiddick Island, the Cape Poge lighthouse was precariously near the edge of the bluff. In January, 1987 the Coast Guard picked the light up with a helicopter and moved it back to safer ground. It is still active as is the three lighthouses on Nantucket: Brant Point, Great Point and Sankaty Head. Of the two lights in the Elizabeth Island chain, Tarpaulin Cove is still active but the light at Cuttyhunk was retired many years ago. The Great Point lighthouse at Nantucket was knocked down by high seas in the blizzard of 1978 but was completely rebuilt in 1986. The new tower is automated,powered by solar cells and is designed to withstand any storm nature can send its way.

The Cleveland Ledge Lighthouse is the newest beacon in the Cape Cod area. It was built in 1941 and is situated in the middle of the shipping channel in Buzzards Bay for traffic approaching the southwest entrance to the Cape Cod Canal. *Aerial Photo by the Author.*

Above: Two ships were wrecked on March 13, 1891 at Gay Head on the island of Martha's Vineyard late at night. The bark *U.S.S. Galena* was being towed by the U.S. Navy tug *Nina* when the two ships became lost in the fog. They grounded south of the lighthouse and sounded distress signals. The men from Gay Head who were accustomed to shipwrecks, rigged a hawser to the two vessels and brought 77 men to shore safely. The survivors were sheltered in local homes. The two ships were salvaged but the bark suffered damage to her hull and had to be scrapped. *Photo courtesy of the U.S. Naval Historical Center, Washington, D.C.* **Below:** On February 20, 1893, the four masted schooner *Douglas Dearborn* was totally wrecked in gale winds and a blinding snowstorm on the north side of Cuttyhunk Island, Massachusetts. A heavy sea was running on shore and made a clean breech over the vessel. She soon filled with water and the crew were driven to the rigging. Life Savers worked to bring the nine crewmen ashore. Because of the cold, seven men suffered from frost bite and required medical treatment. The 1,024 ton schooner was on a voyage from Philadelphia, to Portland with a cargo of coal and was a total loss. *Photo from a souvenir postcard.*

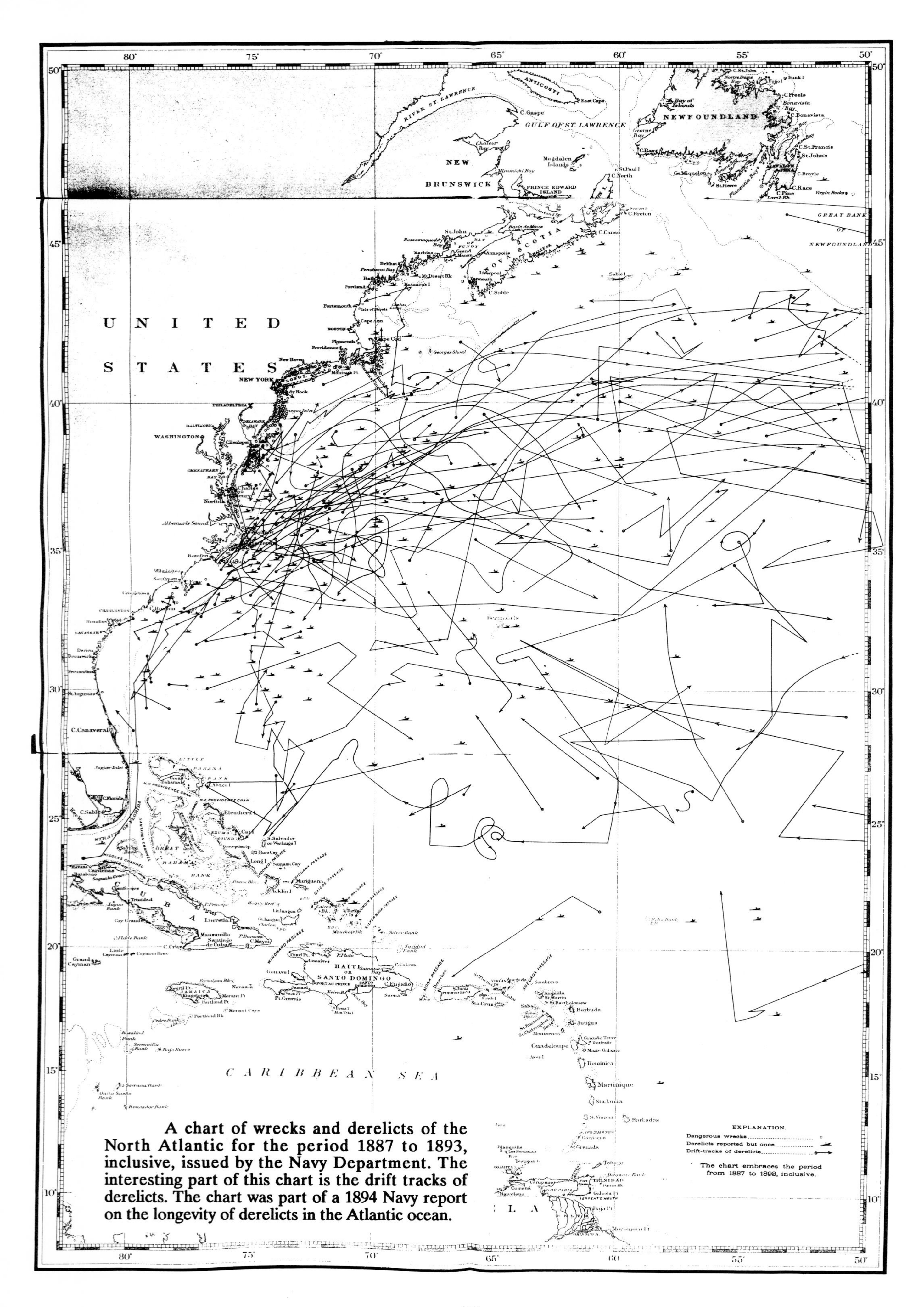

A chart of wrecks and derelicts of the North Atlantic for the period 1887 to 1893, inclusive, issued by the Navy Department. The interesting part of this chart is the drift tracks of derelicts. The chart was part of a 1894 Navy report on the longevity of derelicts in the Atlantic ocean.

The three masted schooner *Messenger* was wrecked at sea off Long Island, New York and the hull floated around for weeks. The derelict washed ashore on December 6, 1894 near Cahoon's Hollow in Wellfleet. *Photo by Henry K. Cummings, Orleans, Mass.*

In the late nineteenth century, one of the hazards to ocean navigation was the many derelicts on the north Atlantic. Wooden sailing vessels were always at the mercy of wind and sea. Frequently storms dismasted these ships and they were abandoned by their crews. The hulls continued to float on their lumber cargoes, drifting aimlessly with the ocean currents, decks awash and constituting a menace to other vessels at sea. The Revenue Cutter service was charged with hunting them down and destroying them or towing them into the nearest port for disposition. The greatest danger posed by the derelicts was when they lay in the path of another vessel, underway at night, or in fog where they could not be seen. Many times this would aggravate matters. When the derelict was rammed by another wooden vessel, an additional derelict was the result. The schooner *Messenger* was wrecked at sea in 1894 and roamed aimlessly off the New England coastline until she came ashore in Wellfleet on December 6. When these hulks washed up on the backside, many of them were reduced to firewood. The Revenue Cutters did other duties around Cape Cod. Many times the cutters came to the aid of vessels aground on the shoals. Often the Life-savers carried lines in their open boats between the grounded vessels and cutters. They also helped set the sails to assist ships in getting underway again.

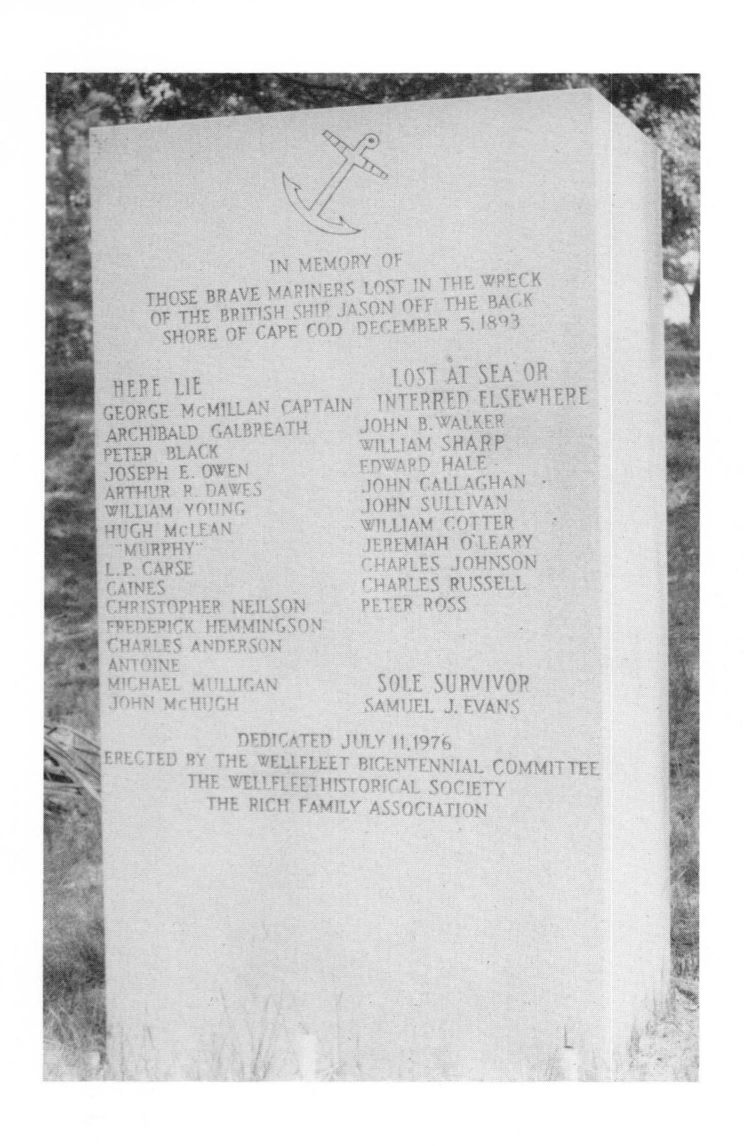

Left: On December 5, 1893, the British Ship *Jason* was wrecked near the Pamet River Life Saving Station with the loss of 24 men. The disaster was described as: "The most disastrous wreck that has occurred within the scope of Life Saving Service operations in recent years." Sixteen bodies were buried in Oak Dale Cemetery in Wellfleet. Officials in the town of Truro had said that the cemeteries in their town were too full and Oak Dale was comparatively new. On July 11, 1976, a monument, dedicated to the memory of these men, was sponsored by the Wellfleet Bicentennial Committee, the Wellfleet Historical Society and the Rich Family Association. American and British flags were placed at the stone by those attending the dedication. The stone lists the names of the men buried at the site and those whose bodies were lost at sea or interned elsewhere and the sole survivor, Samuel J. Evans. *Photo by the Author.* **Below:** This photograph shows the Pamet River Life Saving crew returning from the wreck of the *Jason*. The picture was taken a few days after the surf had gone down to permit the life-savers to inspect the broken hull and to search for any bodies that might have still been aboard. *Photo courtesy of Richard M. Boonisar, Norwell, Mass.*

Early in the morning of May 6, 1896, the schooner *Daniel B. Fearing*, out of Philadelphia for Boston, stranded in thick fog on the beach in Wellfleet, one mile north of the Cahoon's Hollow Life-saving station. The Life-savers launched their boat and after a difficult pull, removed the crew of nine and brought them to safety. The heavy seas continued to pound the vessel until she broke up and was a total loss. The three masted Newport, R.I. vessel was carrying a cargo of coal. *Photo courtesy of Capt. W.J.L. Parker. U.S.C.G. (Ret.)*

Another significant wreck occurred on December 23, 1896 off the coast of Chatham. The four masted schooner *Calvin B. Orcutt* was riding out a northeast blizzard at anchor, just off shore, when she was spotted by Jonathan Eldredge, a fisherman from North Chatham. Eldredge informed Fred W. Nickerson, a former member of the Life Saving Service who knew from experience that the vessel could not ride out the storm. He walked to the telegraph office to inform the keeper of the Orleans station by telegram. Because of the storm, the telephone lines were inoperative at the time. At the telegraph office in Orleans, Mr. Henry K. Cummings volunteered to walk to the home of Superintendant Sparrow in East Orleans to carry the news. Mr. Sparrow was able to reach Keeper Charles at the Orleans station by telephone. He assembled his men and left immediately for the wreck. They arrived at the scene, five miles south of the station, after midnight. The Life Savers had battled snow drifts for the entire distance. The vessel had sunk on the outer bar with only her masts standing and no one in sight. The Life Savers fired a line out but there was no one on board to receive it. The entire crew of nine men had perished in the storm tossed waters. The *Calvin B. Orcutt* was built in 1888 in Bath, Maine and was of 953 Tons. She was bound from Portland, Maine to Norfolk, Virginia and was a total loss. A small bit of the vessel is still visible today in Orleans. Part of the galley was removed from the hull and brought ashore. It was added to another building on Monument Road in Orleans and became part of a house, later to become the "Galley West Gift Shop." In 1897, the Life Saving service erected a new station at the location, five miles south of the Orleans station, where the vessel was lost. The Old Harbor station completed the chain of twelve stations along the backside of Cape Cod between Wood End in Provincetown and Monomoy in Chatham. After the Monomoy disaster of 1902, another station was built at Monomoy Point.

Above: The wreck of the *Calvin B. Orcutt* off Chatham on December 23, 1896 with the loss of all hands was the cause of a new Life Saving Station to be built on the outer beach. The location was five miles south of the Orleans station. The men of that station were not able to save any of the crewmen aboard the four masted schooner because of the delay in notice of the disaster. This station completed the chain of twelve stations along the backside of Cape Cod between Wood End in Provincetown and Monomoy Island in Chatham. *Photo courtesy of Noel Beyle, Eastham, Mass.*
Below: In an effort to save one of the last remaining Life Saving Stations on Cape Cod the National Seashore contracted to have the Old Harbor station moved to Provincetown in order to save it from destruction by an eroding shoreline. The station was loaded on a barge by cranes and towed to the Cape tip where it was later moved to safe ground and is now a museum. *Aerial Photo by the Author, plane piloted by the late Richard C. Kelsey, Chatham, Mass.*

Fishing schooners frequently met with disaster on the backside of Cape Cod. These vessels were powered by sail and the only aids to navigation were the compass, charts and a sounding lead. Georges Bank is the most productive fishing ground off the east coast of the United States. It is located one hundred miles east of Cape Cod. With a full fare of fish, the captain of a vessel usually set his course due west and hoped to make Highland Light his first landfall. More experienced mariners could often tell their location by taking soundings on the way to port and checking the type of bottom sand found on the lead. Coming in off the grounds was dangerous in bad weather. Exact positions could not be determined without a landmark and many fishermen grounded on the backside when they were out of their reckoning. The wrecks were moved by the tides, higher up on the beach and lay forgotten until summer when they became the locations for happy picnics and curious sightseers.

The United States Life Saving Service continued to aid the stranded fishing vessels along the back shore of Cape Cod but often there were others involved. The legendary Mooncussers were gone but the wreckers sometimes seemed to frustrate the efforts of the men in the Government service. There was a small village at the end of Monomoy Point, south of Chatham. The residents were engaged in wrecking. The narrow channels around the point caused many a vessel to go aground or be totally wrecked. The Monomoy Life Saving Station was located about two and one half miles north of the point. On May 8, 1899 the fishing schooner *Thomas Brundage* was lost in the fog and ran aground on Shovelful Shoal south of Monomoy Point. The crew from the Monomoy Station went to the aid of the grounded vessel but were not needed. In the wreck report filed in Washington, Keeper William T. Tuttle stated: "No assistance required of Life Saving Service after the arrival of our boat. A bargain with the wreckers had been made to put the vessel afloat. It seems to be the policy of the wreckers to reach a vessel as soon as possible and conclude a bargain before we can get there, and as about nine tenths of the strandings occur near Monomoy Point the wreckers have all the advantage of distance. They can reach a vessel ahead of us every time in spite of our best endeavors. This station has always labored under a great disadvantage in that respect, the greater part of our work has been away off at arms length with nearly always wreckers to compete with." The wheels of bureaucracy turned slow as the new station at Monomoy Point was not established until 1903.

The ships that sailed the world's oceans underwent a gradual change during the second half of the nineteenth century. The days of the wooden sailing ships were ending. Ultimately, with the arrival of the 20th century, iron and steel were predominant in new ship construction. The beautiful days of sail had passed by and the sight of a full rigged ship with all sails set, with the wind on her quarter and the bone in her teeth were almost gone. A few of the coastal schooners continued to carry cargoes but could no longer compete with the newer ships powered by steam engines, fired by coal, maintaining a dependable schedule. Some of the sailing vessels worked during the 1920's but, by 1930, most of them had been laid up in the backwater creeks abandoned and rotting. The Life Saving Service, the Revenue Cutter Service and the Lighthouse Service all combined to provide greater safety for ships at sea but the disasters continued along the backside of Cape Cod.

Above: The great gale of November 26-27, 1898 was named the Portland Gale by New Englanders after the steamer *Portland*, was lost with all hands during the storm. The photo above is a copy of a painting by Wallace Randall that hangs in the Marine Museum at Fall River, Massachusetts and depicts the steamer at sea during the storm. It was estimated that nearly 200 persons lost their lives when the ship went down. The gale wrecked over 150 ships on the eastern seaboard. Wreckage from the *Portland* came ashore along the backside of Cape Cod. All telephone and telegraph communications were knocked out by the storm. Officials on the Cape transmitted news of the wreckage ashore to France from the French Cable Station in Orleans. From there it was sent to New York over another cable and thence to Boston over telegraph wires. **Below:** Some pieces of the *Portland* washed ashore in Orleans. This picture was taken around the first of December, 1898. Standing with the wheel of the *Portland* and other pieces of the ship is Captain Rufus Snow. The location of the photograph is at the corner of Main Street and Tonset Road in Orleans. *Photo from the Author's collection.*

Above: The two masted schooner *Robert Byron,* bound from Rockport, Maine to Providence, R.I., with a load of lime ran aground near Race Point in Provincetown in dense fog. Men of the Life Saving service boarded her and tried to save the vessel but she was badly hogged and began to leak. When the water reached the lime, fire broke out on the schooner and she burned to the waterline. The vessel was a total loss but the crew were saved. *Photo from a souvenir post card.* **Below:** The multitude of Marine traffic along the back side of Cape Cod is evidenced by this photograph taken around the turn of the century from Pochet Island in the southeast section of Orleans. There are eighteen two, three and four masted schooners along the horizon and all except one appear to be headed north. The logs of several ship watchers along the coast show that this is not a large number. *Photo courtesy of William Payson, East Orleans, Mass.*

CAPE COD POST CARDS

For almost as long as there have been tourists, there have been post cards. There are thousands of post cards advertising the tourist attractions of Cape Cod. The first cards were made through the photographic process and were sharp and clear reproductions. The later cards were screened half tones and were not as clear. Several of the very early post cards of the Cape were photographs of the Life Saving Service stations and of the men during drills. One of the most popular was the lifeboat drill. There were many different pictures of the launch and recovery of the lifeboats. The breeches buoy drill and the station facades were among the other widely used subjects. In addition to the Life Saving Service, the lighthouses were the other favorite views on the cards. Shipwrecks were pictured on scores of different cards and it is perhaps, significant, that the practice is still popular today. When the *Eldia* was driven ashore on Nauset Beach at Orleans, in March, 1984, a dozen different post cards appeared on the market within two weeks of the grounding. Most of these are now collectors items.

The Start of the Life-boat, Cape Cod

Pictures of the Life-Savers in action were among the best sellers in the post cards on Cape Cod. The scene above shows the men hauling the surf-boat to the beach. The scene below is the life-savers with cork life-jackets, launching the boat into the ocean during the "Surf Boat Drill."

Surf Boat Drill.

Two more views of the surf-boat taken in sequence with the one on Page 42 showing the boat underway and the recovery of the boat from the water, using one horse power and seven man power. The card on the bottom is a classic error in the title. The drill is actually the Breeches Buoy Drill. The cards were copyrighted in 1908 by H.I. Robbins in Boston, Massachusetts but were printed in Germany.

The top card is one of hundreds printed with the photograph of a Life-saving Station. This one, however, contains another error in the title. The station was always known as the Race Point Station, not Race Pond. The center card is one of the early shipwreck cards with a photograph of the *Onondaga* pictured on the front. The ship stranded on Nauset Beach in Chatham on January 13, 1907. The card on the bottom is another view of the *Onondaga* being unloaded by Orleans men prior to her being hauled off the beach in March 1907.

The top card was found in a flea market and has no identification other than what was written on the front: Cuttyhunk, Mar. 29, 1907. It shows the stern of a broken schooner near the rocks. The center card shows three barges stranded on the beach in North Truro on April 4, 1914. One of these vessels was saved. The other two were burned but the deck house of the *Coleraine* (bottom card) was hauled up to the top of the cliff and converted to a pro-shop for the Highland House Golf Links. Nine holes, 2,362 yards and a magnificent view.

THE CUTTYHUNK DISASTER

Early in the evening of February 24, 1893 the Canadian Brig *Aquatic* was wrecked on Sow and Pigs reef, off Cuttyhunk Island, the southernmost of the Elizabeth Chain. The brig was of 361 tons bound from Sugua, Cuba, to Boston, Massachusetts with a cargo of sugar. The captain of the vessel made distress signals which were seen on Cuttyhunk. The signals were not visible from the Life-Saving station at the other end of the island, two miles away but the Light-house keeper dispatched a messenger to inform them of the wreck. A crew of six volunteers of the Massachusetts Humane Society launched a boat to go the aid of the stricken vessel. The mission proved to be an impossible one and five of the six men were lost when the heavy seas overturned their boat beside the brig. The crew of the brig managed to save one man from the lifeboat crew but all the rest were lost. A boat from the Life Saving Service arrived at the wreck about two hours later but the keeper decided to return to the island and wait for daylight as the vessel was laying easily and not in danger of breaking up.

Nothing of the disaster was known on shore until the next morning when a body of one of the crewmen washed onto the beach. The men lost were Frederick A. Akin, Isaiah H. Tilton, Hiram S. Jackson, Eugene Brightman and Timothy Akin, Jr. The only man saved was Josiah H. Tilton. Three of the bodies washed ashore and two were never found. The disaster was reported in newspapers all over the nation and a fund drive raised over twenty-six thousand dollars which was turned over to the Mass. Humane Society for distribution to the wives and children of the men lost. The fund contributed to the immediate needs of the families and later provided educational monies for the children.

The Massachusetts Humane Society boat in Chatham with some men posing with what looks like a small model sailboat in the lower right hand side of the photograph. The Humane Society boats were manned by volunteers when they were available to rescue shipwrecked sailors.

The framework of the windmill on Nantucket Island was built from timbers salvaged from shipwrecks along the shores. They were cut and fitted to make an octagonal framework and then double planked much like a ship. The miller was usually a retired seaman, acquainted with sails and rigging. This knowledge was an advantage in running the mill. *Photo by the Author.*

Among the unique historic buildings on Cape Cod are the windmills. A few of these old structures have been restored and are open as tourist attractions. The old mills have been on the Cape for over 200 years and have a connection with the sea. Henry David Thoreau in his mid-19th century wanderings along these outer shores described the windmills: "The most foreign and picturesque structures on the Cape, to an inlander, not excepting the salt works are the windmills...gray looking octagonal towers, with long timbers slanting to the ground in the rear, and there resting on a cart wheel, by which their fans are turned around to face the wind. They looked loose and slightly locomotive, like huge wounded birds, trailing a wing or a leg, and reminded one of pictures of the Netherlands."

The mills were situated on high hills in almost every town. Their lofty perch caught the gentle breezes to turn the vanes and grind grain grown by the local farmers. In good weather, these land ships with their sails turning served as positive landmarks for ship masters navigating around Cape waters. The sails attached to the vanes on the windmill had to be rigged similar to the ones on board a ship. When the wind velocity increased, the sails had to be furled to prevent damage to the structure. Many millers were former sailors who were well versed in handling sails. The windmill was controlled very similarly to a ship in that the winds determined the operation. When the wind died, the windmill, like the ship, was becalmed. The windmill on Nantucket was erected in 1746 by Nathan Wilbur. Timbers from shipwrecks were cut and fitted to make the octagonal framework then double planked with oak, much like a ship and covered with shingles. While in operation, the mill turns a large stone grinding corn to meal. The Nantucket folks relate that the meal has a distinctive flavor and it makes fantastic muffins.

A wave conceals the hull as it moves toward the Nantucket Lightship on her station, fifty miles southeast of the island. Twenty foot seas are not uncommon at that location. *Photo courtesy of the National archives.*

Chapter Four

In the early part of the nineteenth century, additional aids were needed to supplement the country's lighthouses. Because of the myriad of shoals and sand bars surrounding Cape Cod, navigation was sometimes a nightmare. Shipwrecks were frequent. It was not always possible to locate fixed lights in the areas where they were needed. The problem was solved with a floating lighthouse, anchored near the shoals. One of the first outside lightships was placed at Sandy Hook, New Jersey near the gateway to New York City in 1823. In a few years, lightships were stationed on both the Atlantic and Pacific coasts. The largest concentration of these vessels was around Cape Cod. In 1922, there were ten stations between Buzzards Bay and Nantucket Shoals. Nine of these vessels were all within sight of land but the Nantucket Shoals lightvessel was stationed fifty miles at sea. It was one of the most exposed and dangerous stations in the Lighthouse Service. The crewmen aboard the Nantucket lived a fitful existence. Life was at best monotonous; at worst perilous. During storms, the tossing motion of the vessel was nauseating while in thick fog the thundering noise emanating from the fog-horn made any sleep impossible and simple conversation intermittent.

Life aboard a lightship around Cape Cod was not considered the best duty in the service but in the summer it was not all that bad. During the warm months of the year there were few storms to contend with and the crew could fish, read or play cards when not on watch. At the Cross Rip station in the middle of Nantucket Sound, the men enjoyed daily visits by the island steamships on their passage from Woods Hole to Nantucket. Periodically the steamer would stop to drop a bundle of newspapers for the lightship crew. This action provided them with reading materials and let them catch up on the latest news. In the winter, conditions changed with the weather. During storms the vessel rocked, pitched and rolled. Added to this was the constant worry of collisions during fog. Most of the crewmen were, however, conditioned to the rugged life aboard a light vessel.

The lightships were usually anchored in unprotected positions to mark dangerous shoals and reefs. In stormy weather the light had to stay bright with the fog horn sounding at the prescribed intervals for the vessel to fulfill its purpose. The exposed locations of these light-vessels was the cause of several collisions. In 1904 the Lighthouse Board reported seven cases of damage to their lightships from collisions with barges under the tow of tugboats. The most serious was the Pollock Rip vessel No. 47 off Chatham. She was hit in dense fog by a barge in tow of a tug owned by the J.B. King Transportation Company of New York. Her false stem was torn off causing her to leak considerably. The light vessel was towed to New Bedford for repairs and was back on her station a week later. There were other collisions suffered by the Shovelful Shoal and Cross Rip light vessels, causing minor damages. There were numerous other hardships encountered by the lightship men. One was the shortage of supplies during prolonged stormy conditions. Stores on a lightship have to be replenished every two months because of space limitations. When the supply ship couldn't reach the lightship, the men had to live on hardtack and water for the duration until the weather abated.

Above: The schooner *Montauk* was driven ashore by gale winds near Brant Point on Nantucket Island on November 26, 1900. The vessel remained upright and lay on the beach high and dry until she floated without damage during another gale on December 4th. *Photo courtesy of Charles F. Sayle, Nantucket, Mass.* **Below:** The three masted schooner *Jennie C. Mae*, with a cargo of coal was wrecked on the eastern end of Peaked Hill Bars on February 7, 1902 due to an error in navigation. Life Savers from the Peaked Hill Bars and High Head stations removed the crew by surfboat the following morning. Salvage attempts were made by tugboats but the vessel was a total loss. *Photo courtesy of John Bell, Provincetown, Mass.*

Above: The Handkerchief Lightship station was half way between Monomoy Point and Great Point on Nantucket. The station was in service from 1858 to 1951 to insure safe passage for sailing vessels through the dangerous shoals in the area. **Below:** The Hedge Fence Lightship station was half way between Cape Cod and Martha's Vineyard Island. The station was in service from 1908 to 1933 and stood vigil over a long slender sand bar running parallel with the passage over the shoals. *Photos courtesy of the Shore Village Museum, Rockland, Maine.*

The Lighthouse Tender *Azalea* rescued the crew of the Nantucket Relief Lightship number 85 when she sank during a storm in December, 1905. *Photo courtesy of the Shore Village Museum, Rockland, Maine.*

At the turn of the century a young man from Italy was experimenting with electric and magnetic waves. Guglielmo Marconi was sending signals across open spaces without any wires. At first it was 20 miles, then 100 and then 200. By using more powerful equipment he was able to increase the distance. The ultimate goal was to send his wireless signals across the Atlantic ocean. Long electromagnetic waves were used as signals. When transmitting long distances, extremely high voltage was required. On January 18, 1903 messages were exchanged across the Atlantic. The first two-way communications were between President Theodore Roosevelt and King Edward VII. The radio station was located on the outer shores of Wellfleet on Cape Cod. The European station was located at Poldhu, England, while a third station was located at Glace Bay in Nova Scotia. Marconi's success with the new apparatus signaled the opening of a new industry.

The vast potential of radio wireless for maritime communications was soon realized. Ship to ship, and, ship to shore messages, of news and weather reports soon filled the airways. The new radios were purchased for use on Government vessels to transmit weather and other operational information. It was not long before another use for the equipment was realized. In December, 1905 the Relief Lightship Number 85, was battling a roaring northeaster on the Nantucket south shoals when a leak developed in her hull. The crew bailed and the storm grew worse. Captain Jorgensen ordered the radio operator to send word over the wireless that they were sinking and needed help. The untested equipment was their only hope and they were not sure if they were being heard. The signals, however, were received by the lighthouse tender *Azalea*. She left New Bedford and headed east into the storm. She arrived on scene the next day and could barely make out the battered lightship through the thick snowstorm. Through skillful maneuvering, the crews managed to rig a hawser between the two vessels. Captain Charles I. Gibbs of the *Azalea* advised the crew of the lightship to abandon their vessel. They launched their lifeboat and went aboard the tender. The *Azalea* left for New Bedford with the lightship in tow. A short time later the hawser parted and the small light vessel turned over on her starboard side and sank. The Marconi apparatus was credited with the first contribution to a rescue at sea.

Above: The Pollock Rip Lightship station was moved from time to time but remained substantially in the same area seven miles off Chatham. At one time the station name was SLUE. This vessel was the number 73 lightship and in 1925 was placed on the Vineyard Sound station. She was lost on September 14, 1944 during a hurricane with her entire crew. **Below:** The Nantucket Lightship No. 117. This vessel was cut in half on May 15, 1934 by the Cunard White Star liner *Olympic*, while on her station, fifty miles southeast of the island. Five men were lost in the accident.

Above: The trauma and tragedy surrounding a shipwreck is graphically illustrated in this view of wreckage on Nantucket. It was probably a heavy storm that broke up the vessel to the condition seen in the photograph, contrasted by an idyllic summer scene with three girls and an elder friend. The only flaw in the photograph is the movement of the dog's head. *Photo from the collection of Paul C. Morris, Nantucket, Mass.* **Below:** The fishing schooner *Elsie M. Smith* from Gloucester, Massachusetts came ashore on the beach at Orleans during thick weather and snow squalls on February 10, 1902. Three members of her crew launched a dory in heavy seas and were capsized by the heavy surf. Only one man managed to swim ashore, the other two were lost. The wreck was discovered shortly afterwards and the men of the Life Saving Service were on the scene. The breeches buoy was set up and the remaining crewmen brought ashore safely. *Photo by Henry K. Cummings, Orleans, Mass.*

Above: When the five masted schooner *Arthur Seitz* was launched in 1901 in Camden, Maine she hung up on the ways. She had to be blocked up and the ways realigned in order to properly launch her. The old salts said that she was hoodooed by christening with flowers instead of breaking a bottle of wine over her bow and this jinxed her from the start. At that time, the state of Maine was dry and no alcoholic beverages could be sold. *Photo courtesy of Capt. W.J.L. Parker, U.S.C.G. (Ret.)* **Below:** Apparently the jinx stuck with the vessel as on May 25, 1902, the *Arthur Seitz* was wrecked on Skiff Island Reef. Her wreckage washed up on Tuckernuck Island near Nantucket. *Photo from the marine collection of Frank E. Claes, Orland, Maine.*

Above: Just after midnight on September 18, 1902, the schooner *Dora Mathews* stranded on Monomoy Island, south of Chatham. Life Savers rescued the crew but the Captain refused to leave his vessel. The cause of the wreck was listed in the wreck report as: "Captain being worse for liquor." Crewmen reported the officers being drunk and unable to con the ship. The schooner proved to be a total loss. *Photo courtesy of Capt. W.J.L. Parker, U.S.C.G. (Ret.)* **Below:** The Barkentine *Albertina*, bound from New York City to her home port of Windsor, Nova Scotia, collided with an unknown obstruction in Pollock Rip Slue at midnight on July 1, 1904. The collision broke a hole in the forward part of the hull and her master ran the vessel aground on Chatham bar to prevent her from sinking. The crew were all saved but the barkentine was a total loss. *Photo from the collection of Joseph A. Nickerson, Chatham, Mass.*

The two masted schooner *E. Arcularius* came ashore on Naushon Island during a storm on November 14, 1904. Lightkeeper Carson and Postmaster Robinson of Tarpaulin Cove rescued Captain Nelson and his crew of three men using a flat bottom, fourteen-foot skiff. The civilian life-savers made two perilous journeys with the small boat through heavy surf to rescue the crew of the schooner. In the photo above, there is a salvage vessel alongside the schooner. *From the collection of Frank E. Claes.*

A January blizzard stranded two schooners in Cape Cod Bay in 1905. The *Alice Mae Davenport* (above) of Bath, Maine and the *Harwood Palmer* (below) of Boston, Mass. Both vessels had anchored to ride out the gale but the anchor chains parted, and the ships went aground. The four masted *Davenport*, 300 yards off North Dennis, and the five masted *Palmer*, 200 yards off Yarmouth Beach. The two schooners were caught in winter ice and could not be hauled off until late March. The *Davenport* was hauled off on March 21, 1905 and the *Palmer* was refloated on March 24th. *Photo of the Davenport courtesy of the Maine Maritime Museum in Bath, Maine. Photo of the Harwood Palmer courtesy of Matthews C. Hallett, Yarmouthport, Massachusetts.*

Above: The three-masted schooner *William Marshall* was caught in a gale on December 7, 1906 and lost all of her sails. The next day she became waterlogged and was abandoned by her crew. After her crew left the vessel was manned by a salvage crew. When seas became rough this second crew had to be removed by the Revenue Cutter *Gresham*. On December 11th the schooner washed up on the beach a mile north of Highland Light and became a total loss. The vessel had been bound from St. John, N.B. to New York City with a load of lumber. *Photo by Charles H. Jennings, courtesy of Harold B. Jennings.* **Below:** The small fishing schooner *Lavonia* went ashore during the night in thick rainy weather at Nauset Beach in Eastham. The vessel was a total loss despite the efforts of her crew and the Keeper of the Nauset Station to save her. The grounding occurred on July 30, 1905 during the inactive season for the Life Saving Service. The schooner was on her way in from Georges Bank with a fare of fish when lost. One of her masts was cut down and used for years after as a flag pole in front of the town library in Eastham. *Photo courtesy of Howard W. Quinn, Eastham, Mass.*

Above: The Nova Scotia schooner *G.M. Cochrane* came ashore in a storm on November 4, 1906, three miles south of the Nauset Life Saving Station. The vessel was discovered at 5:25 a.m. and with the seas breaking over the stern, the life-savers rigged the breeches buoy and landed the crew of six. Storms drove the vessel farther up on the beach where she lay for more than a year. She was sold at auction and later salvaged. She went back to sea under the name of *Albani. Photo courtesy of Charles F. Sayle, Nantucket, Mass.* **Below:** The fishing schooner *Buena* came ashore near the Race Point Life Saving Station in Provincetown on January 7, 1908 during a strong southwest rainstorm. The Wood End Life Saving crew tried to launch their boat but the surf was too high. The schooner's crew of 17 landed in their dories and were assisted out of the surf by the Life Saving Crew. The *Buena* was a total loss. *Photo courtesy of Arthur Bickers, Provincetown, Mass.*

Above: The Boston fishing schooner *Mattakeesett,* while bound in from the banks with 20,000 pounds of fish, went ashore on Peaked Hill bar on March 5, 1911. Captain Parsons and two crewmen were capsized in a dory but were rescued by Surfman Oliver of the Highland Life Saving Station. The remainder of the crew were all rescued. The vessel lay on the sand like a beached whale and ultimately became a total loss. *Photo by the late Admiral Donald B. MacMillan, Provincetown, Mass.* **Below:** The Canadian schooner *Mizpah,* on a passage from Lunenburg, N.S. to Boston with a cargo of potatoes was wrecked at Peaked Hill Bars on December 2, 1909. Three crewmen were washed overboard when the schooner drove on the bars. Four other crewmen were rescued by the Life-saving service crew from the Peaked Hill Bars station. The vessel was a total loss. *Post card from the collection of Clive Driver, Provincetown, Mass.*

A reproduction of a painting of "The Rescue" by Marshall Johnson. The forty-foot motor boat succeeded in removing the crew of seven men from the three masted schooner, *Charlotte T. Sibley* grounded off Bass River at Yarmouth on October 7, 1907.

THE RESCUE

On the stormy morning of October 7, 1907, Captain Hatch of the three-masted schooner *Charlotte T. Sibley* decided to anchor and ride out the storm. The vessel lay with both anchors out, off the mouth of Bass River in Nantucket Sound, off the coast of Yarmouth. With the increase in wind came further stress on the anchor chains and soon the port chain parted. Two hours later the starboard chain broke and the schooner was carried on to the bar. The position was precarious and it wasn't long before waves began to break over the vessel, driving the crew into the rigging. The location of the wreck was a critical factor in that the nearest Life Saving Station was on Monomoy, about ten miles away. Another consideration was the time involved to advise the Government Life Savers of the wreck and any delay would mean the loss of her crew. The *Charlotte T. Sibley* measured 140-feet in length, with a 32-foot beam and a depth of 11 feet. She was 376 gross tons.

Charles H. Davis, a summer resident of South Yarmouth, called out his crew of four and left Bass River in the forty-foot motor yacht ILDICO to go to the aid of the schooner's crew. The small vessel left the river into the teeth of the gale and anchored beside the grounded schooner, a half mile off shore. The men aboard the sailing vessel left the rigging and lowered a small boat near the bow. They all made it aboard safely and drifted down to the waiting yacht. The crew aboard the ILDICO heaved a line to the small boat and hauled it alongside. The seven men were taken on board and brought ashore safely. The *Charlotte T. Sibley* was later salvaged and she sailed until February 22, 1919 when she foundered in the middle of the Atlantic ocean. All of her crew was saved when she sank.

Above: The U.S. Naval auxiliary training ship *Yankee* went aground on Spindle Rock in the western end of Buzzards Bay on September 23, 1908 while on a cruise for midshipmen. The vessel was hard up on the rocks and was not refloated until December. *Photo from a souvenir post card.* **Below:** The *Yankee* was floated on December 4th but sank in Buzzards Bay while being towed to New Bedford and was declared a total loss. *Photo courtesy of Mystic Seaport Museum, Mystic, Connecticut.*

On January 23, 1909, in dense fog, 26 miles southwest of Nantucket Island, the Italian liner *Florida* collided with the British White Star liner *Republic*. This photograph was taken from the rescue steamer *Baltic* on the day following the collision by Mr. A. Henry Savage Landor, a passenger. The photo was printed in Harpers Weekly. The canvas patch on the side of the vessel was to slow the inrush of water but the ship later sank.

On January 22, 1909, the 15,378 ton White Star Liner *Republic* left New York City bound for the Mediterranean with 700 passengers and crew aboard. The next morning the vessel was steaming through dense fog and zero visibility. At 5:45 a.m. whistles sounded and the ship lurched as the Italian steamer *Florida* collided broadside with the *Republic*. The ship was cut down through three decks. Six men were killed when the ships collided. The boiler room flooded almost instantly and the fires were doused to avoid an explosion. Lights went out all over the vessel as several passengers left their cabins in their night clothes while others were without shoes. The *Florida* stood by as the crew lowered lifeboats. The *Republic's* radio operator, Jack Binns, found his shack had been heavily damaged in the collision but the wireless was still operable. Without the ship's power, however, he had to hook up to batteries to begin sending the CQD distress signals. On Nantucket Island, the radio operator at Siasconsett answered the distress call and asked "All right, old man, where are you?" Binns transmitted the message from the Captain: "Republic rammed by steamer 26 miles southwest of Nantucket Lightship. Badly in need of assistance, but no danger to life. Capt. W.I.Sealby."

The Siasconsett radio quickly relayed the message to nearby revenue cutters and other ships that were in the area. The steamer *Baltic* was passing the Nantucket Lightship at the time, when her radio operator intercepted the distress call and reported to Captain J. B. Ransom. The message: "Republic dangerously injured, Lat. 40-17 N.,Lon. 70 W." Captain Ransom ordered a change in course to go to the collision site. The passengers were leaving the Republic in lifeboats and going aboard the *Florida* but that ship was crowded and her decks were full of survivors. Everyone was cold and hungry, wondering if they were all going to be lost if the ships sunk. The *Florida* with a weakened bulkhead forward was taking on water but seemed to be in little danger of sinking as long as the collision bulkhead remained intact.

Above left: The noted hero of the *Florida - Republic* disaster was Jack Binns. He was the wireless operator aboard the White Star Liner, who stuck to his radio key, directing the rescue ships to the scene. The rescue of the 700 persons aboard the stricken ship was credited to the endurance of Binns and his radio. *Photo reproduced from Harpers Weekly.* **Above Right:** Following the thrilling rescue of the passengers and crew of the *Republic,* medals were issued by the passengers to the crewmen of the three vessels; *Republic, Baltic* and *Florida* commemorating the event. The obverse pictured the steamer *Republic* with a hole in her side with the letters "C.Q.D." denoting the radio distress signal at that time, sent out by Jack Binns. The reverse carried the date and purpose of the medal. *Photos by the Author.*

The *Baltic* arrived at the position given by radio but the dense fog made it impossible to see any trace of the other two ships. The radios crackled with new locations. All afternoon Captain Ransom searched for the damaged ship but could not find her. Circular currents were carrying the vessels away from the initial spot of impact. Rockets were fired, whistles were blown and bells rung but the effort seemed to fail until they made contact in the early evening. Upon locating the *Republic*, Captain Ransom took off most of her crew and three thousand bags of mail. Then they set out to find the *Florida*. The Italian vessel was not far away and for the rest of the evening and through the night the lifeboats transported survivors to the *Baltic*. At dawn the fog dissipated and revealed that many other vessels had answered the call. The *Republic* was taken in tow by Revenue Cutters but she sank a couple of hours later. Capt. Sealby and Mate R.J. Williams were rescued out of the water by the cutter *Senaca* and taken to New York where, along with Jack Binns, they were given a tremendous welcome. An outpouring of admiration followed and Jack Binns became a world figure. He had stayed with his wireless set to the last and as a result, 1,650 passengers had been rescued at sea.

Above: The granite lighters *Benjamin Franklin* and *Potomac* were driven ashore at Sandwich in a northeast gale on November 9, 1909. The two lighters with 23 crewmen on board were part of a group of vessels engaged in laying a breakwater for the new Cape Cod Canal. The vessels were a total loss. *Photo by Small, courtesy of the Bourne Historical Society.* **Below:** The Marine News for the port of Hyannis reported that on December 7, 1909, "the schooner *Katherine D. Perry* was in a collision with the Pollock Rip Lightship No. 47 on her station, east of Chatham, Mass. The lightship was raked fore and aft, carrying away both masts, lantern box and gear, bow stove in and doing other damage. The *Perry* made no stop and proceeded to Vineyard Haven for repairs." The Lighthouse tender *Azalea* towed the Relief Lightship to the Pollock station to replace the damaged vessel.

Chapter Five

After the turn of the century the decline of the commercial sailing vessel continued. American sailing ships had, since the mid 1800's been prominent on the world's oceans. One of the foremost shipbuilders of the day, Donald McKay, built 32 clipper ships in Boston between 1850 and 1869. Eight small clipper ships were built and launched at the Shiverick Shipyard on Quivet creek in East Dennis in the 1850's. Others, like the packets, the down east windjammers and finally the multi-masted coastal schooners, contributed heavily to this country's economic boom. The British tramp steamer helped to retire the merchant sailing ships and dominated world commerce into World War One. During the war, there was a short period of resurrection for the sailing vessels but this only delayed the inevitable. Most of the tall masts were cut down and some of the old wooden hulls were tethered in groups of three or four behind seagoing tugboats. The barges only lasted a few more years and, as John Masefield wrote of the windjammers: "They mark our passage as a race of men, earth will not see such ships as those again." Cape Cod's sea captains were legend on the world's oceans. They sailed the seven seas and made their fortunes. When they "swallowed the anchor," they retired back home on the Cape. Some of the old mansions on Cape Cod were erected by these men. The designs were copied from other large houses the world over. They brought the drawings back home and built their homes. Most of them still stand today and are considered architectural masterpieces by some while others share different views. When asked the style of the Captain Penniman house in Eastham, a National Park Ranger replied: "Nineteenth century awful".

Life aboard a Cape Horn square rigger was not often the adventure depicted in the novels and modern day motion pictures. The hard times experienced by mariners have been outlined most dramatically in the many books written by those who lived on board and kept diaries. The fo'c'sle sailor in the deep water square rigged vessels frequently had to suffer from harsh treatment by some of the mates. Added to that was the incessant calls for "all hands" to trim or set sails while being slammed around in the Cape Horn fury. It was usually every hour round the clock. Furling rock hard canvas in freezing temperatures molded the man's character while hardening the calluses on his hands. Most of the food served on board tended to assuage the hunger but did nothing to please the palate. When the sailors returned home, however, it was the good times that were remembered. While spinning yarns to awe the younger generation, mystical legends were created from their adventures. These obviously suffered some embellishment to impress the listeners and to inflate the ego of the person narrating the tale.

Some of the more prominent sailing vessels around Cape Cod were the multi-masted sailing schooners. The three masted schooner evolved around the early to mid 1800's and with the increasing economic growth the need for larger vessels became evident. The next step was the four master in the late nineteenth century. The normal sailing route for the coastal merchant schooners came north through Vineyard Sound, over the shoals south of the Cape and out through Pollock Rip Slue, north along the backside of Cape Cod and around Provincetown and thence to Boston, Portland or the Maritimes. The economic boom at this period created a need for larger ships to carry bigger cargoes. Later the five and six masters were built. Conspicuous along the Cape Cod horizons during this time was the four master. There were 458 of these work-horses built along the Atlantic and Gulf coasts. The dubious attraction around Cape Cod for these vessels was that twenty of them were totally wrecked here. Of the fifty-seven five masters built, seven of them were wrecked, sunk or burned off Cape shores. And of the ten six masters, four of them were wrecked in Vineyard and Nantucket sounds.

Above: On January 23, 1910, the six masted schooner *Mertie B. Crowley* was wrecked on Wasque Shoal, three miles south of Chappaquiddick Island of the eastern end of Martha's Vineyard Island. The huge vessel was bound from Norfolk, Virginia, for Boston with a cargo of 4,796 tons of coal. She had encountered heavy weather for the entire trip and was off her course when she stranded on the shoal. A spectacular rescue was made of the persons aboard the schooner by Captain Levi Jackson of Edgartown and his crew with the fishing sloop *Priscilla. Photo courtesy of Charlie Sayle, Nantucket, Mass.* **Below:** The *Mertie B. Crowley* broke up and part of her wreckage washed up on Muskegat Island. The part in the photograph may be part of the stern. *Photo from the collection of Paul C. Morris, Nantucket, Mass.*

An heroic rescue took place off Martha's Vineyard in January 23, 1910. This time it was a group of civilians who answered the call. The six masted schooner *Mertie B. Crowley* was bound from Norfolk, Virginia for Boston with a cargo of 4,796 tons of coal. The vessel had a registered tonnage of 2,824 gross tons and was 296.5 feet long. She was built in Rockland, Maine in 1907 and her master was William H. Haskell. The schooner had encountered heavy weather for her entire trip north from the coal port. She lay to for over a day while south of Long Island, New York because of the dense fog. When the vessel got underway again she was out of her reckoning and mistook the light on the south coast of Block Island for Montauk Point. Early the next morning while sailing northeast she struck on Wasque Shoal, about three miles south of Chappaquiddick Island on the eastern end of Martha's Vineyard.

The stormy weather continued with high waves breaking over the grounded schooner. The heavy seas swept away all of her boats and pounded the vessel without mercy. Captain Haskell rushed to his cabin to save his wife. Mrs Haskell quickly grabbed what clothes she could and then aided by her husband, climbed into the fore rigging where the crewmen lashed her to the crosstrees. The Captain and the remaining thirteen crewmen all sought safety in the forward part of the rigging with the Captain's wife. Later, at ten o'clock in the morning the ship broke in two. The stern settled into deeper water. Fortunately the crew were all forward. The wreck was sighted at nine o'clock by watchers in Edgartown harbor. It was several miles from any Life Saving Station and no time to wait for the arrival of a Government surfboat crew.

Quickly, Captain Levi Jackson and three of his crewmen, brothers Henry and Patrick Kelly along with Louis Doucette started the engine on the 37 foot fishing sloop *Priscilla* and headed out of the harbor to effect the rescue of the people aboard the *Mertie B. Crowley*. The trip was not without event as the seas were still running dangerously high and it was a twelve mile trip to the scene. The sloop arrived late in the afternoon and anchored in the lee of the wreck. The fishermen braved the rough waters and launched three dories to remove the survivors. Mrs Haskell was first lowered down from the crosstrees. She leaped into a dory and was taken to the sloop. One by one, the crewmen all jumped into the small skiffs. All except one completed the transfer successfully. The steward missed the dory and dropped into the sea. Patrick Kelly grabbed the man, reached out and held onto the jib-boom rigging until he was assisted in the rescue by his shipmates. The fifteen survivors and four crewmen were a heavy load for the small sloop in the rough seas but Captain Jackson succeeded in making safe harbor and landing the survivors on the shore. The townspeople aided the survivors and cheered Captain Jackson and his crew. The giant six masted schooner *Mertie B. Crowley* was a total loss.

The greatest tragedy in modern maritime history occurred on April 14, 1912, when the steamer *Titanic* struck an iceberg, 400 miles southeast of Newfoundland and sank two hours later. Over fifteen hundred persons lost their lives in the disaster, only seven hundred and six survived. The loss was reported in the annual report of the Life Saving Service and comparison made on the losses in the service. "Nothing can better assist one to comprehend the vastness of this, the most appalling maritime tragedy of the age, than the statement that the number of persons who perished when the steamer went down exceeded by nearly 200 the total number of persons lost within the field of the Life-Saving Establishment since its organization - a period of more than forty years." In September 1985, the wreckage of the *Titanic* was located by an expedition from the Woods Hole Oceanographic Institution. The hull was found by two remote control submersibles at a depth of approximately 13,000 feet.

Above: On Aug. 11, 1911, the three masted schooner *Theresa Wolf* went aground on Chatham Bar early in the morning. The crew of the Old Harbor Life Saving Station launched their surfboat and went to the schooner. Four crewmen and three passengers were landed by the life-savers along with their personal belongings. **Below:** Local wreckers came out to the schooner shortly after dawn but the vessel was full of water and was a total loss. *Photo courtesy of Noel Beyle, Eastham, Mass.*

Above: Seventeen men were lost on January 10, 1911 when three barges were wrecked on Peaked Hill Bars in Provincetown. The *Pine Forest, Corbin* and *Treverton* were in tow with the tug *Lykens.* The tow left Philadelphia on January 6 and ran into a northest storm with 60 m.p.h. winds. The towing bridle became undone and the tow was lost. The only wreckage found was that of the *Pine Forest* which washed up on the beach but the crews were all lost. The only piece of the *Treverton* ever found was the stern section with the name. *Photo courtesy of Clive Driver, Provincetown, Mass.*
Below: The schooners were involved in various accidents all along the east coast. The *John Paul* was in a collision off Savannah, Georgia and her bow was demolished. The jibboom was snapped off and set back aboard. On January 13, 1914 the tern schooner sank during a storm in Nantucket Sound, four and one half miles southeast by east from the Hedge Fence Lightship. The Revenue Cutter *Acushnet* tried to tow the vessel to port but the storm had finished her. *Photo courtesy of John Fish.*

One of the giant coal schooners was wrecked in a storm on Tuckernuck Shoal off Nantucket on December 5, 1914. The *Alice M. Lawrence*, bound light from Portland, Maine to Norfolk, Virginia, was reported to have ran up on the wreck of the schooner *French Van Gilder*, which had been wrecked on the same spot twenty-nine years earlier. The *Lawrence* broke her back on the other wreck and was a total loss. *Photo courtesy of Charles F. Sayle, Nantucket, Mass.*

A second large six-master was lost off Cape Cod on December 5, 1914. The *Alice M. Lawrence* was bound from Portland, Maine, to Norfolk, Virginia, in ballast. She hit the wreckage of the *French Van Gilder* on Tuckernuck Shoal in Nantucket Sound. The *Van Gilder* had been wrecked on the same shoal twenty-nine years earlier and was loaded with paving stone. Wreckers had hoped to save the *Lawrence* but she had broken her back when she ran up on the remains of the other vessel. The *Alice M. Lawrence* had a gross tonnage of 3,132 and was built in 1906 at Bath, Maine. Her home port was in Portland, Maine. These multi-masted schooners were owned by several people in the Maine cities. Local newspapers there reported the accidents no matter where they occurred. The Bath Daily News for Monday evening, December 7, 1914, carried the following article:

"STORM CAUSES HAVOC ALL ALONG THE ATLANTIC COAST."

"An unidentified war ship believed to belong to a foreign navy foundered after going ashore on the coast of Delaware during the gale. Six masted schooner *Alice M. Lawrence* in bad fix in Nantucket Sound. Nantucket Light Ship torn from moorings and likewise a small schooner in harbor of refuge in Point Judith.

"Boston Mass., Dec. 7 - The southerly storm which first made itself evident on the New England coast this Saturday was raging relentlessly today and up until noon, had caused three marine disasters, all accidents were not accompanied by loss of life. The Schooner *Alice M. Lawrence* ..of Portland grounded in Nantucket Sound. The schooner lay well upon the shoal with about seven feet of water about her. She is reported to be badly hogged and local mariners believe she will never be released from the grip of the sand. The position of the *Lawrence* off the Tuckernuck Shoal is considered precarious as great seas prevented any near approach by life savers. Dec. 17...schooner first stripped and then left to her fate. Resting on wreck of sunken vessel, hope of saving vessel given up owing to her back being broken."

A deck view of the *Alice M. Lawrence*, taken as the salvors were picking up all of the usable gear from the hull. Wreckers took all of the rigging and other items of value which could be sold. The vessel was a total loss. *Photo courtesy of Charles F. Sayle, Nantucket, Mass.*

Above: On January 30, 1915, the tug *Watuppa* towing a barge through the newly opened Cape Cod Canal struck a washout near Bournedale and sank with her bow on the canal bank. The vessel was salvaged by a wrecking tug from Boston and was in service into the 1940's. **Below:** A rare photograph taken aboard the barge *Manheim* while she lay aground in front of the Highland Station in Truro. This vessel was one of three barge cast ashore in a storm on April 4, 1915. The *Manheim* lay on the beach for one year before she was pulled off and then went back into service. In the photo, the Life Savers are dressed in white except for the keeper. The three barge crewmen and their Captain (in derby hat) posed with the Life Savers on deck. Some important detail of an early schooner barge can be seen around the men. *Photos by Small, courtesy of the Bourne Historical Society.*

Above: On July 9, 1915, the Metropolitan Line passenger steamer *Bunker Hill* crashed into the schooner *Abbie Bowker* of Thomaston, Maine. The schooner was enroute from New York to Friendship, Maine with a cargo of coal. The accident occurred during heavy fog in Vineyard Sound near Tarpaulin Cove. The steamer was not damaged but the *Abbie Bowker* lost her bow sprit, figure head and most of her head gear. The damage was all above the water line and the schooner proceeded to Vineyard Haven for repairs. *Photo from the collection of Frank E. Claes, Orland, Maine.*
Below: The schooner *Cora M.* with a cargo of lumber, out of Charlottetown, Prince Edward Island, for Vineyard Haven, was wrecked off Monomoy Point in a sixty mile gale on September 16, 1917. The Coast Guard rescued the crew of four men. The schooner floated on her cargo. Her wreckage washed ashore on Monomoy Island. The Monomoy wreckers stripped her. *Photo courtesy of Noel Beyle, Eastham, Mass.*

Above: The Muskegat Island Life Saving Station was established on January 11, 1883 with Capt. Thomas S. Sandsbury as keeper. This was one of the first order stations with an enclosed lookout tower. This station burned to the ground on December 27, 1889. The loss was valued at $5,000. **Below:** A new, larger station was built on Muskegat Island in 1896 to replace the previous station lost to fire in 1889. The Life Saving Service had rented quarters for the crew in the interim. *Photos from the collection of Paul C. Morris, Nantucket, Mass.*

Above: The crew of the Muskegat Station during a lifeboat drill. The five men propelled the boat with pulling oars while the keeper steered. Note the cork life-jackets on each man. In the bow, an oarlock enables the keeper to steer from either end. **Below:** After the Life-saving service acquired motor driven lifeboats, life became easier for the surfmen. Long hours of tedious rowing were relieved by the internal combustion engine. This is the Muskegat power lifeboat underway. *Photos from the collection of Paul C. Morris, Nantucket, Mass.*

The United States Congress enacted legislation in 1914 to improve the government rescue teams on land and sea. On January 28, 1915, President Woodrow Wilson signed the Coast Guard act, which merged the Revenue Cutter Service and the Life Saving Service into one unit. The Revenue Cutter Service was established in 1790. The Life Saving Service was a collection of congressional acts dating from 1848. These operations were incomplete and scattered for many years. Corrective legislation was enacted but formal institution did not occur until 1878. The work of life saving along our coastline was carried out by both services operating as separate organizations. Crews of the Life Saving stations and Revenue Cutters often cooperated in rescue work. These involved extensive duplication of effort. The consolidation increased the efficiency between the shore and sea units.

The obligations placed on the Coast Guard weighed heavily and their responsibilities were enormous. The annual report for the fiscal year ending June 30, 1915 outlined some of the various duties falling on this service: "Warnings to vessels running into danger, medical and surgical aid to the sick and injured, recovery and burial of bodies cast up by the waters, extinguishing fires at wharves, dwellings, and business structures and fighting forest fires; cooperating with local authorities in the maintenance of public order and apprehending thieves and other lawbreakers; preventing suicide; restoring lost children to their parents; recovering stolen property and salving miscellaneous articles from danger or destruction; acting as pilots in cases of emergency; furnishing food, water, and fuel to vessels in distress; protecting wrecked property, and furnishing transportation and assistance to the branches of the public service." This would seem to indicate that any duty not specifically assigned to any other branch of the military came under the aegis of the Coast Guard, and was ultimately carried out by them.

The steamer *Bayport* grounded in the Cape Cod Canal on December 14,1916 after breaking loose from a tug. A salvage attempt was made but the vessel sank and blocked the canal for three months until engineers used dynamite and blasted her into pieces. *Photo courtesy of Robert H. Farson, Yarmouth, Mass.*

The Coast Guard as organized was a part of the military forces of the Government. The military system of the former Revenue Cutter service was utilized as a foundation for the organization of the Coast Guard. This required many changes in the status of the former Life Saving service personnel. That service had no retirement benefits for its members. The transfer of personnel of the Life Saving service to the Coast Guard was accomplished by issuing appointments as Warrant Officers and Petty Officers to the former Keepers and Number one Surfmen. Prior to the establishment of the Coast Guard, the Life Saving Station Keepers and their Number One Surfmen enjoyed excellent employment status and tended to keep their jobs well past the age of sixty. When the Coast Guard appointments were made, a majority of these men took advantage of the new benefits and applied for immediate retirement.

On Good Friday, April 6, 1917, war was declared. The German submarines had been sinking U.S. ships and the move officially brought America into the World War. The entry by the U.S. tipped the advantage over to the Allies and on November 11, 1918, the Armistice was signed and the war was over. Cape Cod did not escape the noise of war. On the foggy Sunday morning of July 21, 1918, a periscope broke the calm surface of the Atlantic waters three miles off Orleans. The *U-156* surfaced and started shelling a tug and her tow of four barges. The barges were sunk and the tug set afire. There were some injuries to her crew but no one was killed in the engagement. The one sided battle between the submarine and the barges was the subject of Cape gossip for weeks. The tales of the incident that have been passed along were exaggerated more with each telling. It was a fact that these were the only enemy shells to land on American soil in World War One. But numerous other rumors spread about a possible invasion, spies on Cape Cod aiding the Germans and some dud bombs that were dropped by Navy planes from nearby Chatham Naval Air Station. Following the attack, coastal patrols were strengthened and the Navy acquired new exploding devices for their aerial bombs. There was, however, some after effect of the incident. The late Sumner A. Towne of Buzzards Bay, Editor and Publisher of the Independent, heard about some shady operations that went on following the submarine attack and wrote an essay, using the vernacular of an old time Cape Codder, as part of his continuing series on early legends of Cape Cod and entitled:

.....As Eye See It.....

THE CAPE COD HUCKSTERS... My Uncle, Japeth Snow, was a Coast Guardsman down to th' Orleans Station back in 1918. That were back in th' days when th' world was fightin' World War I......an' th' time when th' German Submarine sank them three barges off Orleans. Oh, that created quite a stir back then.

O' course, everybody got some thrilled over th' whole thing, after th' first fear o' invasion wore off an' folks down t' Orleans an'Eastham an' Chatham an' Wellfleet got bit by th' souvenie bug. 'Fore you knowed it everybody wanted a piece o' one o' them barges as a keepsake.

Wellsir, it was th' fellers in th' Coast Guard Station who sort o' reaped th' harvest! Bein' as how they was right there on th' beach, all th' time they had good opportunity t' corner th' market on th' wood what come ashore from them sunk barges an' they was sellin' off pieces o' plankin' fer the dangdest prices.....an' makin' a good haul. Then, folks from up th' city way heard about it an' they come down t' Orleans t' get a war souvenir too! My goodness, Uncle Jape (we allus called him Uncle Jape) he was gettin' downright rich on th' barge wrecks. He allus tol' us that he got th' best prices f'r th' wood with th' shrapnel from the German shells imbedded in it. "Make y'rself ten dollars a chunk on shrapnel wood!" He'd allus say.

Now, o'course, there was a time when all th' wood finally run out.....an'th' demand was still there as big as ever. Uncle Jape said that really put him in a quandry on account of he could see all that souvenir money comin' in...but all th' barge wood had run out.

One mornin' he was goin' through th' rescue shed when he spies th' big Lyle Gun sittin' in th' corner waitin' for th' next shipwreck. Now, th' Lyle Gun was a small cannon that was used t' fire a line out t' a stranded ship so's the crew could be brought ashore by breeches buoy. A little while later he was walkin' out back o' th' station an' he noticed that th' ol' iron stoves they'd had in th' station kitchen was bein' thrown out an' they was settin' in th' yard waitin' t' be carried off. Then, that afternoon out on th' beach he found two big hatch covers washed up on shore probably from some passin' schooner what lost 'em overboard in a recent gale.

Wellsir, them stoves an' them hatch covers an' that Lyle Gun started t' go 'round an' 'round inside Uncle Jape's head until he couldn't think o' nothin' else. Pretty soon he went an' got Charlie Sears an' Oz Mayo an' tells them what he's found.....

Oz an' Charlie got a cart an' brought up th' hatch covers from the beach an' dumped 'em out behind th' station. Uncle Jape went an' wheeled out th' Lyle Gun t' where Oz an' Charlie dumped th' hatch covers an' then they all went into th' tool shed an' come out with three sledge hammers. Well, they set to on them stoves with a real slam an' a bang an' afore you knowed it they had them ol' stoves broken down into small bits an' pieces. Then they charged up th' Lyle Gun with powder an' rammed in some chunks o' stove ...aimed th' Lyle Gun at one o' th' hatch covers an' ....blaaamm! .....they touched off th' Lyle Gun.

They did this two - three times....an' 'fore you know it they had themselves a whole bunch o' wood with shrapnel imbedded all over it. They broke up th' hatch covers into small pieces...an' then and there...they was right back in th' souvenir business...for a couple o' more weeks at least.

T' this day....they's a lot o' souvenirs o' th' only German attack on American shores during World War I down t' Wellfleet an' Orleans an' up in th' city what were really just hunks o' an' ol' hatch cover blown full o' busted up stoves.

Uncle Jape an' Oz Mayo an' Charlie Sears made a lot o' money on that deal an' proved themselves t' be th' first o' th' Cape Cod Souvenir hucksters.

Leastwise, that's th' way eye see it!

The Provincetown fishing schooners *Valerie* on the left and *Comorant* were driven ashore in a gale during the winter of 1918. Both vessels were salvaged and returned to the fishing grounds. *Photo from an old post card.*

The sprawling Chatham Naval Air Base on Nickerson Neck which was beyond the present day Eastwood Ho Country Club. The base was used only during World War One and was shut down soon after the war ended.

THE CHATHAM NAVAL AIR STATION

In August 1917, construction began at Nickerson Neck in Chatham on a new U.S. Naval Air Station. The facility was commissioned in January 1918 and the first flight took off on June 6. The base cost seven million dollars to build. The mission stated was the protection of the coastline from Montauk Point at the tip of Long Island, New York, to Cape Ann, Massachusetts. The aircraft consisted of flying boats and lighter than air blimps. HS-2L seaplanes maintained the patrol near shore while the offshore waters were covered by the blimps. After the war, in 1920, the base went on inactive status. It closed up completely in 1923. The air station was headlined in the newspapers twice in its brief career. During the submarine attack off the coast of Orleans in 1918, two planes were launched to engage the U-boat but the bombs did not explode. The submarine left the scene and was not seen again. The second occasion in print was more positive than the first.

On May 8, 1919, three large Navy flying boats, the NC-1,NC-3 and the NC-4 took off from the Naval Air Station at Rockway, Long Island, New York headed for Trepassey, Newfoundland in an attempt to be the first planes to cross the Atlantic Ocean. Their ultimate destination was Plymouth, England via the Azores. The first stop was to be at Halifax, Nova Scotia. The NC-4 lost an engine soon after departing Long Island. Later a second engine threw a connecting rod and the plane had to make a water landing in the ocean, eighty miles east of Cape Cod. She taxied all night and the next morning arrived at the Naval Air Station in Chatham. Repairs were made to one engine but the other had to be replaced. The late George Goodspeed of Chatham, a local mechanic, was called to the air station to help install the engine on the plane. The NC-4 left Chatham on May 14th and flew to Halifax. Thence on to Trepassey, Newfoundland. The three planes left Trepassey on May 16th. The NC-4 landed at Horta in the Azores on May 17th at 1:23 p.m. They had flown 1,200 nautical miles in fifteen hours and 18 minutes with an average speed of 78 knots, aided by a 15 knot tail wind. The other two NC planes did not complete the flight to the Azores and had to ditch a few miles short of their destination. The crews were rescued by ships stationed out along the route. The NC-4 flew into Lisbon, Portugal and then to Plymouth, England where they were greeted by the Lord Mayor at "Plymouth Steps", a slab planted to commemorate the spot from which the Pilgrims departed for America 300 years before. Thus, with a repair stop at Cape Cod, the NC-4 completed the first transoceanic flight and one of her pilots was Lt. Elmer F. Stone of the U.S. Coast Guard.

Above: The Chatham Air Station was host to a famous aircraft in May of 1918. The NC-4 stopped at the outer end of Cape Cod for some repairs on two engines which failed while about 90 miles off shore. The plane was headed for Newfoundland to begin the first flight across the Atlantic Ocean. *Photo courtesy of Robert Hardy, Chatham, Mass.* **Below:** The plane was recently restored by the Smithsonian Institution. She is on display at the Naval Air Museum in Pensacola, Florida which is open free to the public. *Photo by the Author.*

Above: The steamer *Ruby* went aground off Madaket on Nantucket on February 4, 1918. There was 1,700 barrels of oil aboard which had to be unloaded before the vessel could be pulled off. *Photo courtesy of Charles F. Sayle, Nantucket, Mass.* **Below:** The steamer *San Jose* rammed the four-masted schooner *Governor Powers* on September 11, 1918, near Half Moon Shoal in Nantucket Sound. The vessel rolled over on her beam ends and was towed to shoal waters for salvage but proved to be a total loss. There was $50,000 damage to the steamer. *Photo by Bob Beattie, Belfast, Maine.*

Above: In August of 1919, the crew of the tug *Ballew* was ordered to bring the vessel to Maine from Philadelphia. The skipper, while on a weekend leave, met a pretty school teacher and invited her along for the trip. The young lady accepted the invitation with the provision that she be back in time for the school opening in September. While underway, the skipper went below for coffee and left the teacher at the wheel, with orders to keep on course. The *Ballew* was headed for Cross Rip Lightship in Nantucket Sound when she got off course. The amateur helmsman had seen a cute little sail boat and wanted to get closer for a picture. When she veered off course the tug went hard aground on Hawes shoal. The outcome of the grounding was the loss of license for the skipper. The tug was pulled off the shoal with the help of a salvage company. *Photo by Bob Beattie, Belfast, Maine.* **Below:** Marine accidents were common along Cape Cod and the planes at the Chatham Naval Air Station had their share of mishaps. It appears to have been a spectacular crash. *Photo courtesy of Robert Hardy, Chatham, Mass.*

Above: On November 24, 1919, the two-masted schooner *Oakwoods* was sunk following a collision with the U.S. Navy submarine R-3 in Buzzards Bay near the entrance to the Cape Cod Canal. The sailing vessel was bound from New York for Bar Harbor with a cargo of coal. The lighthouse tender *Anemone* took the schooner's two man crew to New Bedford. The submarine was not damaged and continued on her voyage to New London, Connecticut. The photograph shows wreckers raising the hull for salvage, using a large floating crane. *Photo by Bob Beattie, Belfast, Maine.* **Below:** The four masted schooner *James Slater* was bound from Liverpool, Nova Scotia to New York on December 21, 1919, with a cargo of wood pulp. A snow storm iced up her rigging and the vessel became unmanageable. Early in the morning she struck the outer bar of Nauset Beach in Eastham. Because of the high seas, the Coast Guard was unable to launch a surf boat. They fired a shot line out and with this were able to land Captain James L. Publicover and his crew in a dory, by making repeated trips, hauling it back and fourth with a tractor. *Photo courtesy of Dolly G. Newcomb, Nova Scotia, Canada.*

Above: During the days of prohibition, rum runners were abundant around Cape Cod. The *Mary Langdon* was anchored a couple of miles east of Nobska Lighthouse off Woods Hole, with a load of lumber piled high on deck, in June, 1925. The Coast Guard asked the skipper to move his vessel out of the path of navigation which he foolishly refused to do. A pre-arranged rendezvous was obvious and the Coast Guard arrested the vessel, moved the lumber and discovered two thousand cases of scotch whisky hidden in the hold. The vessel was seized, the six crewmen arrested and the schooner was towed to New Bedford. *Photo courtesy of the Mariners Museum, Newport News, Virginia* **Below:** A typical rum runner in the 1920's was the fast boat *Nola* The one basic feature these vessels were designed for was speed. The area around the cockpit was built-up for protection of the helmsman. *Photo courtesy of the National Archives, Washington, D.C.*

Chapter Six

The most tarnished era in American history occurred during prohibition. President Hoover called it the "Noble Experiment". Historians refer to it as the roaring 20's. The Volstead act became law on January 16, 1920 and the country dried up temporarily. No alcoholic beverages could legally be sold. There was, however, plenty of illegal whiskey and the underworld became rich dealing in liquor. In the Atlantic ocean, just outside the three mile limit, the bootleggers set up "rum row". A line of foreign vessels loaded with liquor where small, fast boats could run out, load up and speed back to the coast with their contraband cargo. It soon became big business and the men engaged in it became rich overnight. The control of the illegal activities fell to the Coast Guard. The rum runners had fast boats to avoid patrols and the liquor ran free until the Coast Guard acquired speedier launches to compete with the "Black Boats". The rum war continued with both sides trying to outdo the other. There were several wrecks that resulted in many deaths along the entire Atlantic coastline.

What was probably one of the worst disasters during the rum war occurred on December 17, 1927 off the tip of Provincetown. The Coast Guard had acquired some old World War I destroyers from the Navy to catch the rum runners. These vessels were faster than the old cutters and enabled the Coast Guardsmen to fight on somewhat equal footing with the speedy civilian boats. The cutter *Paulding* had completed a patrol and was returning to Provincetown when she was in collision with the Navy submarine *S-4* as she was surfacing near Herring Cove. The converted four stack destroyer hit the submarine amidships cutting down through the hull. The sub sank in 100 feet of water and her crew of 34 men were all lost. The sub was raised three months later and used as an experimental craft in the development of new safety measures for submarines. The new technology was applied a few years later when the submarine *Squalus* sank off Portsmouth, New Hampshire on May 24, 1939 with a crew of 59 men. The rescue efforts were successful and 33 men were brought to the surface alive, utilizing a diving bell. The other 26 men had drowned in the after section of the submarine when it sank. Prohibition ended in November, 1933, when the 21st amendment was ratified and liquor was lawful once again. The Coast Guard had waged a vigorous battle against the rum runners. Neither side could claim a victory, as the experiment of prohibition had failed during the lawless decade. The Coast Guard were outnumbered and could only carry out their duty which they did to maintain the high standards of the service.

The men of the Coast Guard continued to go to aid of grounded vessels on the backside of Cape Cod. But at one time, the rescuers had to be rescued and it took them over a week to get back to their stations. On Friday, January 21, 1921, with a southwest gale blowing, the French steamer *Bacchus* struck on Bearses Shoal at five o'clock in the evening. She lay there for over an hour. The Coast Guards at the Monomoy station launched their surfboat with nine men, under the command of Capt. Dick Ryder. At the same time the Monomoy Point crew of nine manned their motor lifeboat under Capt. Ellis and proceeded to the shoal. The steamer was about a mile and a half from shore. Both boats were lost when they approached the ship. They were swept by the waves and smashed against the side of the vessel. Fortunately the men were all saved by the crew of the freighter and taken aboard. The ship was in ballast and the Captain worked loose from the shoal. He continued on his way to Portland, Maine. There was no convenient way to put the Coastguards ashore so they had to stay aboard the *Bacchus*. The Captain of the freighter was happy to have the them aboard as they were quite familiar with the shoals around Monomoy. They conned the ship into deep water but the two stations on Monomoy were deserted except for the cooks. Other men were called back from leave and still others were transferred to temporary duty so the stations would not be completely unmanned.

The *U.S.S. Swan* became disabled on November 28, 1920, in Cape Cod Bay, while working on a stranded oil barge. The former minesweeper let go both anchors which failed to hold her. She went aground a mile north of Gurnet Point in strong winds and rough seas. Sixty-three persons were brought ashore in a combined effort by Coast Guardsmen from the Gurnet Station, using the breeches buoy and surfboats. The vessel was hauled off the beach on February 21, 1922 by the T.A. Scott wrecking company. The U.S. Destroyer *Mahan,* Cutter *Androscoggin,* U.S.S.*Patapsco* along with men from the Brant Point, Gurnet and Manomet Coast Guard stations participated in efforts to haul the *Swan* off the beach. *Photo courtesy of the U.S. Coast Guard, Washington, D.C.*

The original Palmer fleet consisted of fourteen wooden sailing schooners. Two of these were four masted and the rest were all fives. William F. Palmer was the owner and manager of the fleet and after his death in 1909, bad luck plagued the vessels. They were all lost, one by one, and four of them around Cape Cod. On June 15,1913, the *Paul Palmer* burned off Race Point in Provincetown. On January 12, 1914, the *Fuller Palmer* foundered in a storm off Highland Light. The *Fannie Palmer* collided with the *SS Middlesex* and sank at Great Round Shoal off Nantucket on July 11, 1914. The *Dorothy Palmer* ran on to the western end of Stone Horse Shoal, south of Monomoy Point on March 28, 1923 and was a total loss. She was loaded with 4,000 tons of coal, bound from Norfolk, Virginia to Portland, Maine. The vessel had suffered damage from a northeast gale and had lost some of her sails before striking the Stone Horse. The Cutter *Acushnet* was on the scene to assist but the dangerous sea conditions prevented the rescue. Later when the surf moderated the Coast Guards from the Monomoy Life-boat station removed the eleven members of the crew from the grounded schooner.

The four masted schooner *Gladys M. Taylor* was blown ashore on the shoals, north-northeast of Cross Rip Lightship in Nantucket Sound on November 5, 1921. Bob Beattie, a crewman aboard the tug *Guardsman* made this photograph as she was being pulled free of the sand bars.

Two more six-masted schooners were wrecked in Cape waters in 1924. On January 22, the *Ruth E. Merrill* grounded during a storm and began to leak. The pumps could not stem the flow of water and she began to sink. Captain Johnson ran his ship onto L'Hommedieu Shoals, south of Falmouth, to try and save her. She sank on the edge of the shoal with her decks awash and her masts standing above water. The ship was of 3003 gross tons and was 300 feet long. She had a cargo of 5,000 tons of hard coal aboard, bound from Norfolk, Virginia to Boston. The crew of eleven men landed at Woods Hole in the ship's boat. The vessel and cargo were a total loss. On March 8, the *Wyoming*, the largest wooden schooner ever built, was anchored in the lee of the Cape in Nantucket Sound riding out a storm. The winds picked up to gale force. The vessel was believed to have pounded on the bottom at low tide and broke up in heavy seas on March 12th. Fourteen men were aboard the vessel. There were no survivors. The wreckage washed ashore on the north side of Nantucket the next morning. The *Wyoming* was bound from Hampton Roads, Virginia to St. Johns New Brunswick.

Above: The British freighter *Gaelic Prince* went aground on Round Shoal, off Nantucket on March 31, 1921. Her Captain was unfamiliar with the coast and did not have a pilot on board. The vessel had a cargo of crude rubber, alpaca fiber, jute and 1200 tons of coconut oil in two aft bottom tanks. *Photo courtesy of Charles F. Sayle, Nantucket, Mass.* **Below:** The Coast Guard cutter *Acushnet* was on scene to assist the grounded vessel. She had been driven harder aground when her Captain had tried to back off the shoal against the current. This action built up two large sand heaps under the stern. *Photo by Bob Beattie, Belfast, Maine.*

Above: Five tugs hooked together were pulling on the *Gaelic Prince* to try and drag her off the shoal. Left to Right: *Guardsman, Neptune, Clara A. Doane, U.S.C.G. tug Acushnet and E.J. Morse.* **Below:** The *Acushnet* was connected to the array of tugboats all trying to pull the steamer off. After pumping the coconut oil overboard the ship came off the shoal and steamed off to New York. *Photos courtesy of Charles F. Sayle, Nantucket, Mass.*

Above: The five masted schooner *Sintram*, bound from Philadelphia for Portland, Maine with 3,764 tons of coal came into Muskegat channel between Martha's Vineyard and Nantucket Islands early in the morning of November 15, 1921, bound over the shoals for Pollock Rip. The wind died out and she drifted with the flood tide on to Hawes Shoal. Bob Beattie, aboard the tug *Guardsman* made this photograph on the next day when the tug pulled her out of the sand. She was towed to Vineyard Haven harbor and inspected by divers and on the 18th set sail and headed north again. Early in the morning of the 19th, the steamer *David McKelvy* rammed the schooner in heavy fog off Cape Cod and the *Sintram* went to the bottom. Her crew of 12 men was saved by the steamer. **Below:** A section of a dry-dock broke loose from a tow and stranded on Squibnocket beach at the southwest corner of Martha's Vineyard island. The dock section lay on the beach until December when it was pulled off and towed to New York. *Photos courtesy of Bob Beattie, Belfast, Maine.*

Above: The motor barge *Edith Nute* was wrecked on the outer beach at Chatham on March 27, 1922. Her captain mistook the Chatham Light for the Pollock Rip Lightship. A storm broke up the vessel into several pieces and the wreckage spread out on the beach. **Below:** The broken bow section became a playground for children visiting the beach. The vessel was 187.9 feet long with a 36.6 beam and registered at Boston, Massachusetts. She was built in 1917 at Rockland, Maine.

On March 6, 1923, the relief lightship number 90 struck a rock in Quicks Hole and sank on a ledge. Salvage took months but divers managed to seal the leaks and pump her out. *Photo by the U.S. Coast Guard in the National Archives.*

Shortly after midnight on March 7, 1923, the four masted schooner *Augusta G. Hilton* grounded at West Chop on Martha's Vineyard. The vessel was lost in an easterly gale and blinding snow. The schooner remained stranded for six weeks before being pulled off on a spring tide. *Photo courtesy of the Peabody Museum of Salem, Mass.*

The New Bedford Standard Times reported in the Wednesday, March 7, 1923 edition that the lowest barometer reading in the history of Nantucket was taken that morning at 9:45 a.m. The barometer level was 28.45 inches of mercury. This was accompanied by a northeast snow storm with sleet and hail. Just after midnight the same day, the four-masted schooner *Augusta G. Hilton* dragged ashore one mile west of West Chop at Martha's Vineyard. During the same storm, the Relief Lightship No. 90 was grounded deliberately on Nashawena Island in the Elizabeth chain at the southwest corner of Cape Cod. The light vessel had struck a rock on the west side of Quick's Hole causing the ship to leak. When the rising tide floated the vessel, Captain Arthur S. Berry ran the lightship ashore on Nashawena to prevent her from sinking in deep water. The crew were rescued the next morning by the Coast Guard cutter *Gresham.*

The *Augusta G. Hilton* came ashore in a blinding snow storm and rough seas. She was high and dry for some time. At the time of her grounding, she was bound from Norfolk, Virginia to Boston, Massachusetts. The New York Maritime Register reported on March 21st that: "An attempt to float the *Augusta G. Hilton* was made on the 15th. The Coast Guard cutter *Gresham* and tug *Newport* are working on her." The work proved long and hard as the schooner lay on the beach for six weeks. She was refloated on April 23rd. The *Augusta G. Hilton* was built in 1918 by the Atlantic Coast Company. She was of 1,562 gross tons, 223 feet long with a 41 foot beam. The owner was listed as Crowell & Thurlow, Boston, Mass. After salvage, the vessel sailed until August, 1933, when she burned at sea. Forty-six passengers and crew were removed by the Dutch steamer *Hercules* and landed at San Juan, P.R.

On September 9, 1923, at 3:30 a.m. the steam collier *Everett* rammed the schooner *Frederick J. Lovatt* on the port side abreast the main rigging. The collision cut into the main hatch, down to the keel. The vessels were in Vineyard Sound, three miles east of Hedge Fence Lightship. The crew remained on board atop the after cabin as the ship was towed, decks awash, into Vineyard Haven harbor by Coast Guard cutters. The schooner was raised and towed to Boston two weeks later.

One of the giant coal schooners was wrecked on January 12, 1924, when the *Ruth E. Merrill* grounded on L'Hommedieu Shoal in Vineyard Sound. The vessel had a cargo of 5,000 tons of coal aboard. The twenty-year old ship had been battling a storm and her seams worked open. The pumps jammed with coal dust and could not keep up with the flooding. The schooner was run on the shoal to prevent her sinking in deep water. The crew of thirteen men came ashore at Woods Hole in the ship's boat. The vessel was a total loss. She was one of the largest schooners in the world. *Photo courtesy of the Maine Maritime Museum, Bath, Maine.*

Above: The old schooners and square riggers were cut down to barges as the age of steam power took over on the world's oceans. The tug *Perth Amboy* is shown towing barges 704 and 782 through the Cape Cod Canal in 1916. This tug was shelled and set afire during an attack by a German submarine off Orleans in 1918. **Below:** The largest six masted schooner in gross tonnage was the *Wyoming.* Launched in 1909 from the Percy and Small Shipyard in Bath, Maine, she was 3,730 gross tons, 329.5 feet in length, 50.1 feet in beam and 30.4 feet in depth. She carried 6,000 tons of coal. On March 11, 1924, the vessel was caught in a blizzard in Nantucket Sound and lost with all on board. The disaster occurred at night while the ship was at anchor near the Pollock Rip Lightship. Thirteen men were lost in the tragedy. Parts of the wreckage washed ashore on Nantucket Island. *Photos from the collection of Paul C. Morris, Nantucket, Mass.*

Above: The Gloucester fishing schooner *Evelyn & Ralph* came ashore in dense fog on the south shore of Nantucket on December 6, 1924. When the vessel struck the bar, the foc's'le stove tipped over and set the boat afire. **Below:** After the fire went out the salvage men went to work to save what they could from the wreckage. *Photos courtesy of Charles F. Sayle, Nantucket, Mass.*

Above: The rum runner *Waldo L. Stream* ran on the shoals in Muskegat Channel near Nantucket, on December 26, 1924. There were 2,295 cases of Canadian whisky aboard, half of which was thrown over the side by her crew trying to refloat their vessel. They were all arrested by the Coast Guard and the remaining cargo confiscated. Somehow, the storage place was discovered by local Nantucket residents and much of it "spirited" away in the night. The Nantucket surf finished the hull of the schooner. *Photo courtesy of Charles F. Sayle, Nantucket, Mass.* **Below:** The two masted schooner *Carleton A. Smith* of Portland, Maine went aground on Nauset Beach in Eastham early in the morning of August 10, 1925. The vessel was left high and dry by a receding tide but was pulled off on the evening high tide by the Coast Guard cutter *Gresham.* The vessel had a catch of 54 swordfish and was bound for port when the accident occurred. *Photo courtesy of a friend.*

Early on the morning of January 15, 1925, the U.S. Navy submarine *S-19* grounded near Nauset Inlet off Orleans. The sub lay on the bar for three months until pulled off by a salvage company. The C.G. Cutter *Tampa* lay close to the beach but could not aid the stranded sub. *Photo courtesy of the U.S. Coast Guard.*

Early in the morning of January 15, 1925, the U.S. Navy Submarine *S-19* ran aground off Nauset Beach in Eastham. The sub lay in the surf for three months until finally pulled off by a wrecking company from New York. There was much consternation by the Navy department about the proper salvage technique but an Orleans man had the answer. Capt. Dan Gould was called to Boston by the Navy Department for consultation. His knowledge of local conditions around Nauset Inlet was considered expert by the outer Cape watermen. Capt. Dan boarded the train and when he arrived at the Naval office in Boston he was ushered in to sea a "four striper" as described by the Cape seaman. The officer asked Capt. Gould if he knew the proper way to pull the submarine off the beach without any damage. Capt. Dan pointed out that a hawser should be rigged to the sub, carried off shore to a dead man and through a snatch block. Then back to the bluff where a steady pull during high tides and surf should be maintained. With time, the tide and surf movements would ultimately free the vessel from the sand without any damage. The Naval officer dismissed him without even a thank-you and showed him the door. He returned to the Cape, a little poorer for train fare but smarter by experience. The old Cape Cod sea captain's plan was used to salvage the submarine and the Navy failed give him any credit. But everyone on the outer Cape knew who was responsible for the successful salvage of the *S-19*.

Above: The crew from the Nauset Coast Guard station in Eastham launched a surfboat and rowed out to the grounded U-boat. When within fifty yards of the sub, a huge wave picked up the surfboat and flipped it over spilling the men into the frigid Atlantic waters. The men hung onto the boat and managed to work their way to shore where local people were there to aid them. Other than a dunking, no one was injured. *Photo courtesy of the U.S. Coast Guard.* **Below:** During the period the sub lay grounded, the Coast Guard from the Nauset Station did yeoman service with their motor life-boat. The large cable is shown hanging off the stern of the U-boat.

SUBMARINE SALVAGE OFF EASTHAM

Marine salvage is an uncertain business. The rewards are usually substantial but the risks are great. If the salvor's efforts are successful he gets paid. But if not, he loses everything. It is a job that requires practical knowledge in order to show any degree of success. One of the better known salvage companies was the T.A. Scott Company of New London, Connecticut. Robert Beattie of Belfast, Maine worked for the Scott company as a crewman aboard the tug *Guardsman*. Mr. Beattie, who is now retired recalled that the problems encountered in the salvage were formidable but common sense and ingenuity succeeded where brute strength had failed. He was one of the members of the salvage crew and still has a keen memory of the events that led to a successful salvage.

SUBMARINE S-19 Salvage .... By Bob Beattie

Ashore on Nauset Bar between January and March, 1925, the Navy department worked endeavoring to float her by means of tugs and Coast Guard cutter *Tampa*, but were unsuccessful. The Merritt Chapman & Scott Corp. were called in for consultation and took a no-cure, no-pay contract to float the *S-19.*

The M.C. & S. Corp. sent their wreckmaster and assistants to Nauset to survey the situation. Here, it is necessary to say that a submarine presents complex salvage problems. First there is no deck on a sub upon which to rig salvage gear, consisting of tackles, luff tackles and hauling winch. In addition, the submarine has air tanks and control gear mounted externally on the hull which is easily damaged by contact with other vessels or salvage gear. There were various other problems involved in that there is no place on the hull where a heavy towing or salvage hawser may be rigged, such as the mooring or towing bitts on a cargo vessel. There was also the problem of battery gasses which were taken care of by the Navy men aboard the sub.

To rig a hawser on the sub for a hard pull was a problem. Rigging hawsers girthwise around the hull was not feasible. As she lay in the surf, *S-19* was resistant to surf and sand but very tender with respect to attaching a hawser for a pull, hard enough to move her in the sand. While studying the situation from the beach, the salvors observed that the sub had changed position several times under the action of the surf. There was also much discussion among the local watermen and sightseers regarding eventual salvage of *S-19* and various methods of approach to that end. The M.C. & S. people, experts though they were, didn't discount the value of local opinion and got a lot of opinions and advice.

The surfmen and local watermen knew the sand and surf problem from long experience and the opinion grew and finally crystallized that the *S-19* could best be freed from the grip of the sand by using the action of the surf and a firm constant tension of a hawser rather than by a heavy pull of the customary beach gear. The sub was still subject to movement by the surf at high tide - not solidly set in it. A steady unrelenting tension of moderate force was agreed to be the best approach to the complex problem. And, developed further, the constant tension could best be applied by shore based gear. Toward that end, a plan was developed that included a set of heavy anchors off in deep water, well off shore and a block with a flotation buoy rigged on them. A steel cable would be rigged to the submarine, rove through the block at the anchors and the end carried to shore to a hauling winch upon the bluff.

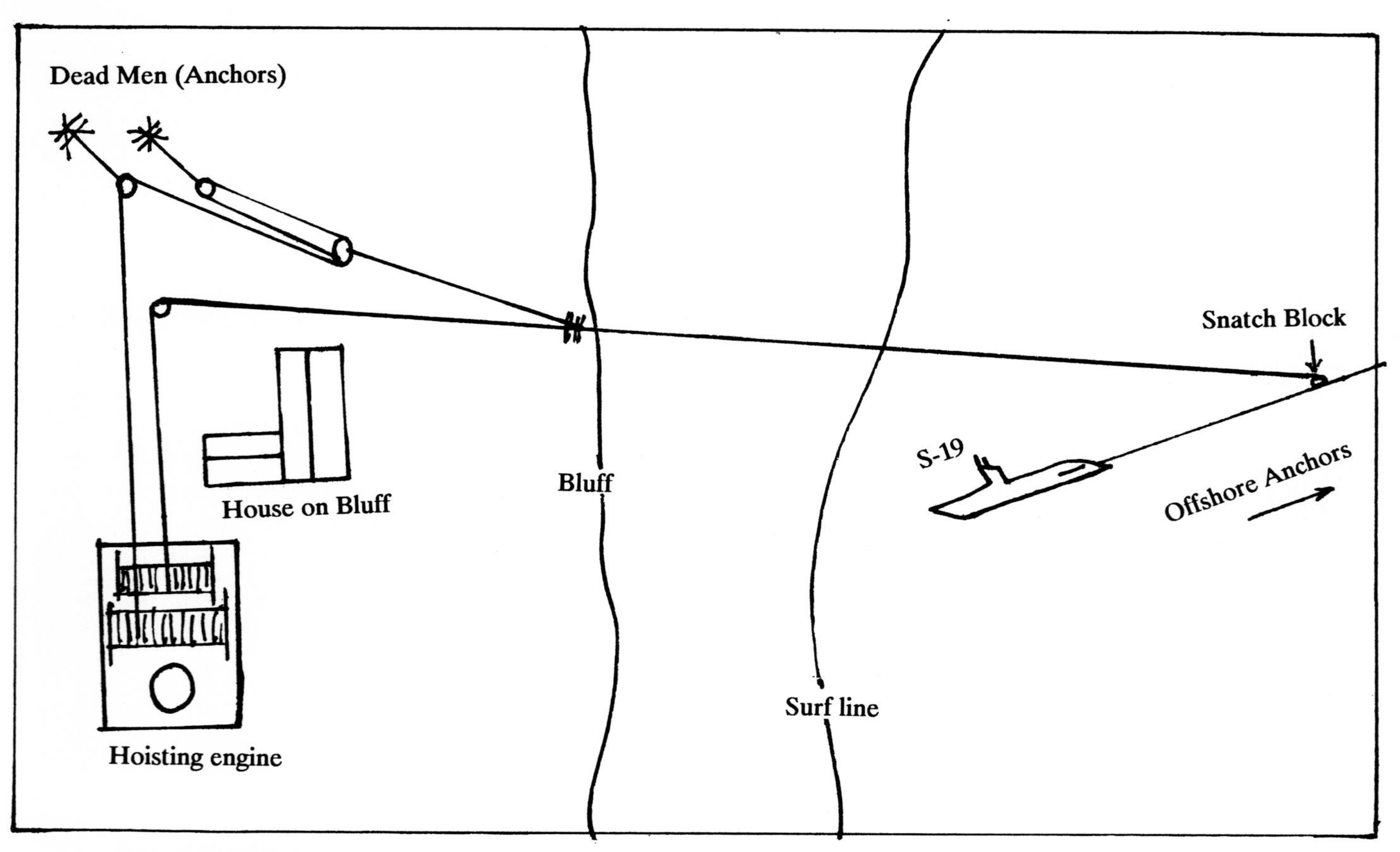

This sketch by Bob Beattie outlines the general arrangement of the deadman anchors, the double drum, twin cylinder hoisting engine and vertical boilers in relation to the long cable stretched offshore and around the snatch block to the submarine.

M.C. & S. had ample heavy salvage gear such as anchors, wire rope blocks, chain and hauling machinery. At New London, two steam boilers and a double drum hoisting engine, water tanks, steam hose, pipe, wire rope and blocks for a 3-fold luff tackle and other gear, fittings and equipment were assembled on a wrecking steamer and sent to Woods Hole. Here the boilers, engine, wire rope and other gear were loaded onto freight cars and sent to Nauset by rail. Local haulers were engaged and the boilers, engine and such moved to the bluff near where the *S-19* was lying in the surf.

The operation called for a very long steel cable, not available "off the shelf". One was made on special order by the American Steel and Wire Company at West Haven, Conn. It was coiled in an open coil on the deck of the lighter EVA at the factory and carried to the beach off Nauset ready to rig. One end was sent ashore by messenger line while EVA was moored off- shore at the anchors. The other end was sent to the sub and made fast to her. The bight of the cable was passed through the heavy snatch block buoyed above the anchors. Up on the bluff the hoisting engine was anchored to a "deadman" and the cable to the submarine secured to one drum and the slack in the cable rove in through the fair-lead block and secured at the fairlead. The hoisting engine was then moved back and the cable payed out until but a few turns remained on the drum, leaving the drum free to heave in perhaps 300 or more feet of cable.

A luff tackle made up of 2-three-fold blocks and 5/8 inch steel cable with a come-along was rigged. One end to a dead-man and the hauling part secured on the second drum of the hoisting engine. The come-along grabbed the main cable to the *S-19* near the fair-lead on the bluff.

Two boilers were set up, one being reserve in the event of a tube failure of the first boiler. Both were connected to the engine although but one was required to furnish steam to the engine. Once set up, the whole operation was exercised in order to work the anchors in and take out any stretch in the dead-men at the fair lead, luff tackle and engine. All was ready for the next high tide, when it was calculated the *S-19* would be nearest to floating. As I recall there was a spell of calm, mild weather at the time of the next moon tide and hope for some easterly weather to go with it.

The Merritt Chapman & Scott company rigged their ground tackle atop the bluff overlooking Nauset Harbor. This photograph shows the buildings housing the boiler, steam drums and the cables running off shore to the submarine. ***Photo courtesy of Fiske Rollins, Orleans, Mass.***

The Coast Guard and heavy tugs with men from them caring for the batteries on the *S-19* along with a wrecking steamer anchored offshore. The Nauset surfboat crew were the only means of communication between the stand-by tugs and the shore end of the operation. Every day they carried the M.C. & S. riggers and wreckmaster to the *S-19* for the purpose of inspecting the cable connections and the Navy man checked on the condition of the submarine. She was not leaking and the hull was not damaged by the surf although at times breaking waves sent spray high above the conning tower. The crew on shore knew little of the conditions out on the *S-19.* We maintained constant tension on the cable by means of the luff tackle and come-along. The tension perhaps amounted to ten tons - not calculated to drag the sub through the sand but to be sufficient to move her ever so little as she moved in the sand as the surf lightened her contact with the beach. There wasn't much action but the cable did come in some from time to time as the surf and high tide combined to lighten her.....We waited for the next moon tide.

It was calculated to move the sub by keeping a fair stress on the luff tackle and at the same time keep the main cable on the engine under tension. If the luff tackle came up two blocks, the engine would pull for all it was worth on the main cable and fleet the luff tackle out for another grab of the come-along, and haul again - but keep hauling move or no. The watch word was 'Hold every inch and that inch too.' Meanwhile, the watches ashore kept up tension on the beach gear and watched.

We boarded not far away from the operation in what I recall a summer boarding house. Ten or so of us, the rooms were unheated but in the kitchen and dining room, life was comfortable. Food was good and plenty of it. There was a taxi man and his beach wagon in on the transportation to town, carrying the mail to the job and the wreckmaster was ever in 'conference' with the local watermen and the life saving station surfmen. Those surfmen did heroic work carrying riggers to inspect the cable blocks and the end made fast on the sub. They must have received some recompense beyond the customary S.S. Pierce 'package' at Christmas. In the end the *S-19* was floated without damage and Navy tugs towed her to Boston.

The Gloucester schooner *Leonora Silviera* came ashore on Peaked Hill Bars circa 1925. The force of the grounding tore her keel out. A smart salvage man bought the wreck and floated her with 500 empty oil drums in her hold. The vessel was repaired and went back fishing again as the schooner *Pilgrim*. *Photo courtesy of Charles F. Sayle, Nantucket, Mass.*

Above: The three masted schooner *W.N. Reinhardt* lost her sails and rudder in sixty-five mile and hour winds during a storm off the tip of Cape Cod on December 7, 1926. The ship grounded at Race Point where the Coast Guard saved the crew of seven with the breeches buoy. The crew was badly frost bitten and were taken to the station for medical attention. The schooner was bound from Albert, New Brunswick, Canada for City Island, New York with a cargo of lumber and lath. Part of her cargo can be seen in the bottom part of the photograph. *Photo courtesy of Allie Ryan, Brooksville, Maine.* **Below:** While the storm raged on for three days the main and mizzen masts came down but the Provincetown wreckers salvaged most of her cargo. The hull was a total loss. *Photo by the U.S. Coast Guard in the National Archives.*

In a blinding snowstorm on February 14, 1927, the Gloucester fishing schooner *Elsie G. Silva* came ashore on the outer Cape Cod beach near Pamet River in Truro. The crew of 20 men abandoned the vessel in five dories. They all made it ashore safely with the aid of the Coast Guard. *Photo by True Fife, Orleans, Mass.*

In the mid 1920's there was a steady decline of ship traffic around Cape Cod but the wrecks continued. In November 1925, the Danish steamer *M.C. Holm.* bound from Boston to New York City rammed the Hedge Fence lightship late at night in Vineyard Sound. The lookout saw the ship on a collision course and alerted the crew. There was barely enough time to lower the lifeboat. The steamer hit the light vessel and she sank in a few minutes. The crew of the lightship refused help from the steamer and rowed ashore to Martha's Vineyard. The vessel was later raised and returned to her station. On March 4, 1927, the Nova Scotia schooner *Montclair* was wrecked on Nauset Beach in Orleans. From a crew of seven, five men were lost. The ship was loaded with wood lath. The heavy seas broke the hull in several pieces and the wreckage with the cargo washed ashore all along the outer beach.

The stamina of the Nauset Coast Guard men was tested on October 16, 1926 when the crew had to row their surfboat twelve miles off shore to rescue crewmen from a burning fishing trawler. A rapidly spreading fire followed an explosion in the engine room aboard the Gloucester based *Pioneer* while she was enroute to the fishing grounds. The fire was spotted by the lookout at the Coast Guard station in Eastham. The crew abandoned their vessel in dories and 14 men were escorted ashore by the Nauset Surfmen. They landed on the Beach in Eastham near the "Outermost House" of author Henry Beston. Mr. Beston gave the men hot drinks before they went to the station. Four other crewmen of the *Pioneer* rowed their dory to the Pollock Rip Lightship. Two of these men were painfully burned in the fire but they were treated aboard the lightship and recovered. Coast Guardsman Yngve Rongner of the Nauset Station told the author, during an interview, of the long row in rough seas and remembered the calluses he had on his hands as a result of the ordeal.

On February 19, 1927, the 75-foot Coast Guard boat CG-238 was on a routine patrol off Plymouth when a northeast gale came up. The vessel tried to make it into Provincetown but was pulled off shore by a strong ebb tide. The engine failed and the crew tried to save their vessel. They anchored off Highland Light all night but strong winds later cast the boat ashore and she broke up with the loss of nine men. The boat had radioed for help but the force of the storm made it impossible for other units of the Coast Guard to reach her. An eloquent description of the storm was written by Henry Beston in his modern classic The Outermost House: "An invisible moon, two days past the full, had risen behind the rushing floor of cloud, and some of its wan light fell on the tortured earth and the torment of the sea. The air was full of sleet, hissing with a strange, terrible, insistent sound on the dead grass, and sand was being whirled up into the air. Being struck on the face by this sand and sleet was like being lashed by a tiny pin-point whip."

Above: On July 20, 1927, two vessels came ashore in the fog at Wellfleet, just opposite the Cahoon's Hollow Coast Guard station. On the left, the schooner *Orleans,* with a load of lumber, lay inside the outer bar. On the right was the fishing schooner *Ruth Mildred* which was headed for Boston with 40,000 pounds of ground fish in her hold. The small two master lay on the beach for a week before being pulled off. **Below:** The schooner *Orleans* was laden with lumber. She was refloated on July 21st and towed to Boston by the cutter *Tuscarora.* On the right hand side of the photograph is the Coast Guard cutter *Henley,* one of the old four stackers employed by the Coast Guard during the period of prohibition. *Photos courtesy of the Cape Codder, Orleans, Mass.*

Above: On December 17, 1927, the Coast Guard cutter *Paulding* rammed and sunk the Navy Submarine S-4 as she came to the surface in the path of the former destroyer. The damage done to the cutter was revealed when the ship was raised on a marine railway at the Charlestown Navy Yard in Boston. The sub was later salvaged but her crew of 40 men was lost. *Photo courtesy of the San Francisco Maritime Museum, San Francisco, California.* **Below:** Following the S-4 disaster, Provincetown residents erected a wooden cross, made from shipwreck timbers, at St. Mary of the Harbor Episcopal Church. The cross memorializes the men lost on the submarine and has their names cast on a bronze plate on the front of the cross. *Photo by Steven Ball.*

Above: On the stormy night of March 9, 1928, the Eastern Steamship liner *Robert E. Lee* grounded on the Mary Ann rocks off Manomet Point in Cape Cod Bay. None of the 263 passengers was injured, but a Coast Guard surfboat from the Manomet Station capsized while returning to the station from the wreck and three of her seven man crew were lost in the high seas. The liner remained on the rocks for seven weeks before salvage crews from the Merritt Chapman & Scott Co., managed to pull her free and tow the ship to Boston. *Photo courtesy of the Mariners Museum, Newport News, Virginia.* **Right:** The citizens of Plymouth erected a plaque dedicated to the three men lost from the surfboat on March 10, 1928. The bronze plaque is attached to a rock situated on a high cliff overlooking Cape Cod bay and the spot where the men lost their lives. They were: Boatswain's Mate William H. Cashman, Surfman Frank W. Griswold and Surfman Edward P. Stark. *Photo by the Author.*

Above: The steamer *West Hika,* bound from Mobile, Alabama, to London, radioed on April 16, 1929 that her rudder had been damaged and she was unable to make port without assistance. She was 270 miles southeast of Nantucket Island at the time. To pass the tow line, a smaller line was floated to the cutter using a life-ring which was picked up with a grappling iron. **Below:** Two thirds of the rudder had been carried away. The cutter *Mohave* arrived on April 18th to tow the steamer into Boston. The weather worsened and the *Mohave* needed help. The cutter *Acushnet* arrived on April 22nd and assisted to bring the *West Hika* into port. They arrived in Boston on the 24th and the steamer had to go into dry-dock for repairs. *Photos courtesy of the U.S. Coast Guard, Washington, D.C.*

Fishing vessels catch fire frequently at sea. The crew abandon their boat and hope to be rescued. This Boston vessel caught fire in the summer of 1929 in Cape Cod Bay between Provincetown and Plymouth after an explosion in her engine room. Her crew was rescued by the fishing vessel *Eleanor. Photo courtesy of Charles F. Sayle, Nantucket, Mass.*

On June 23, 1927, the Clyde liner *Ozark* collided with the steam trawler *Surge* of Boston in dense fog off Cape Cod near Peaked Hill Bars. When the collision occurred the *Ozark* cut the fishing vessel in half and three men were lost and presumed drowned. The trawler sank and the remainder of the crew went aboard the liner, which had suffered damage to her bow. The *Ozark* steamed for shore and was beached in Truro to prevent her from sinking. Captain H.H. Kelly and his crew from the Pamet River Coast Guard station went to the aid of the stricken vessel and ran lines to the cutter *Ossipee.* The cutter pulled the ship off the beach and brought her to Boston for repairs. The *Ozark* was of 2,689 gross tons and 253 feet long, bound from Jacksonville, Florida for Boston, Massachusetts. On July 15, 1927 at four o'clock in the morning in dense fog, the Norwegian freighter *Sagaland* was struck by the Holland-America liner *Veendam*. She sunk five miles off the Nantucket Lightship. After the crash, twenty members of the freighter stepped aboard the *Veendam*. Five members of the crew were picked out of the water and one man was lost. The *Sagaland* sank in thirty minutes.

A needless accident occurred at 12:35 a.m. on June 1st, 1928. The Merchants and Miners freight steamer *Kershaw* collided with the Dollar liner *President Garfield* in Vineyard Sound a few miles east of the East Chop Lighthouse. It was a moonlit night and authorities were at a loss to explain the mishap. The ships had spotted each other five miles apart and each had sounded their whistles to inform the other of their intentions. The first signal was apparently missed by the Captain of the *Kershaw* and at the last minute it was too late. The *Kershaw* was hit on the port side and sank in 72 feet of water with the loss of seven men. Twenty-nine men survived the crash. They were taken aboard the passenger liner and carried to Boston. The *Kershaw* was a total loss.

Above: The Nauset Life Saving Station in Eastham was built in 1872 as one of the first of nine built on outer Cape Cod between Race Point in Provincetown and Monomoy in Chatham. In 1935, the station was visited by Secretary of the Treasury, Henry Morgenthau, when a storm interrupted a party on the outer beach. The lack of basic conveniences moved the Secretary to order a new station to be built. *Photo by Henry K. Cummings, Orleans, Mass.* **Below:** On January 9, 1937 the Nauset crew moved into their new station which was built back from the dunes overlooking the Atlantic Ocean. *Aerial Photo by the Author.*

Chapter Seven

A marine disaster along the Cape beaches has always attracted a large crowd. People have a strange fascination for watching the salvage of a vessel or the rescue of her crew. The accidents that have occurred around Cape Cod were many and varied. Storms wrecked most of the ships but there were several other causes as well. Some ships sank off shore after a collision with another vessel or an underwater obstruction. Running into a derelict or a whale can cripple or sometimes sink a ship. Dense fog is another contributing factor in many maritime accidents. Various other wrecks are blamed on fires, explosions, breakdowns, hull failure and war. Human errors caused many disasters. Crewmen who suffered from illness, exhaustion or injury, sometimes were at fault. Some of the wrecks were caused by laxity or mutiny. The ship disasters often caused death and destruction but the financial hardship to the ship owners was usually covered by insurance.

The second half of the 19th century saw the development of steamboat travel. Regular service was available between most all east coast ports from the Maritimes to Georgia. At that time it was the preferred mode of transportation between coastal cities. The ships were floating palaces of garrish opulence catering to overnight travelers. Double circular stairways with six-foot, hand-carved mahogany newel posts, intricate stained glass windows, velvet settees and Corinthian columns decorated the ostentatious interiors. To this was added luxurious staterooms and ornate dining rooms with lavish menus and impeccable service. To round out the splendor, a spacious grand salon. This all changed after 1900 with the development of the motor car. The first gasoline powered auto was built by Charles and Frank Duryea in Springfield, Massachusetts in 1893. In 1920, there were eight million automobiles in use all over the country. In the 1920's, a favorite pastime for Cape Codders occurred when the Boston-New York steamers cruised through the Canal. The roads were usually lined with automobiles as the night boat passed.

Travel by water declined gradually as highway trucks took freight from the coastal steamers. In 1930 there was an economic crisis in the United States. As the working man tightened his belt, he expected his Government to do the same. The U.S. Coast Guard at this time searched for more cost effective operations. The decline in maritime traffic around Cape Cod was followed by reductions in the number of crewmen employed in the several Coast Guard stations. Three of the lower Cape stations closed completely and never reopened. With the serious economic conditions prevailing, further closings were feared on the Cape. They would ultimately come, but there were, however, other events that occurred to delay the necessary changes. On a delightful summer afternoon in 1935, a sudden thunderstorm caused the Secretary of the Treasury, Henry Morgenthau and a group of friends to seek shelter at the old Nauset Coast Guard station. The distinguished guest was a summer resident of Wianno. He also happened to be the Commander in Chief of the Coast Guard and was greeted warmly by Captain George B. Nickerson. Following a picnic lunch, Captain Nickerson gave his guests a tour of the old station. The Nauset station was one of the nine original Life Saving Stations built in 1872 and was sadly lacking in modern accommodations. Captain Nickerson and Secretary Morgenthau had a long chat and in a few weeks, word came from Washington that a new facility was to be built at Nauset. Subsequently, on January 9, 1937, the Nauset crew moved into a new modern station.

Above: The Peaked Hill Bars Life Saving Station as built in 1872, one of the original nine of this type built on the outer shores of Cape Cod. This building was once owned by Eugene Oneal, famous playright of Provincetown. *Photo courtesy of Clive Driver, Provincetown, Mass.* **Below:** The sea claimed the old Life Saving Station in February, 1931. The Peaked Hill Bars station was a victim of erosion. The building was broken up by the Atlantic surf. It had been long abandoned by the Government and was owned privately at the time of its demise. *Photo courtesy of the Cape Cod National Seashore.* **Bottom:** When the old Peaked Hill Bars station was abandoned, a new station was built along the shore to replace the old one. Some of the shacks in the foreground are summer camps of the era. *Photo courtesy of Clive Driver, Provincetown, Mass.*

Above: The erosion of the beach by the ocean caused the Government to move the station to a new location, back away from the surf. The building was moved from the beach front to a new location and foundation. **Below:** The new location served as long as the station was in commission. The facility was decommissioned the 1930's. *Photos courtesy of Clive Driver, Provincetown, Mass.* **Bottom:** Today, all that is left of the Peaked Hill Bars station is the concrete foundation beside the oversand road used by sightseeing vehicles in the dunes. In the background to the left is one of the service buildings of the station which has fallen down from decades of weather. *Aerial Photograph by the Author.*

Above: A photograph of the crew of the Peaked Hill Bars Life Saving Station during a lifeboat drill. The keeper on the steering oar and the remainder of the crew pulling the boat. **Below:** The crew of the lifeboat coming up the beach after a drill. The boat was hauled on to the cart by the men. The horse then pulled the cart up to the station where it was stored inside. This was an established weekly practice for all thirteen stations along the outer shores of Cape Cod. *Photos from the collection of Clive Driver, Provincetown, Mass.*

Above: During the last part of the schooner era in the 1930's, bits and pieces of wreckage could be seen on most any beach along Cape Cod and the Islands. The wreckage was usually half buried in the sand but, nevertheless, picturesque. This is believed to be the bow of the Gloucester fishing schooner *Governor Fuller,* which came ashore at Coskata on Nantucket Island. *Photo courtesy of Charles F. Sayle, Nantucket, Mass.* **Below:** The Dollar liner *President Hayes* went aground off Monomoy Point near Chatham in dense fog on July 10, 1931. The 10,533 ton steamer was hard up on Shovelful Shoal for two days while the cutter *Mohave* worked to free her. The liner was enroute to Boston but did not have any passengers on board at the time of the grounding. She was pulled off on the 13th and proceeded to Boston. *Photo courtesy of the U.S. Coast Guard, Washington, D.C.*

Above: The Island Steamer *Naushon* altered course to avoid a collision in Vineyard Haven harbor on August 24, 1931, and was caught by 50 m.p.h. winds. The steamer was forced to shore by the winds and a variety of other craft were caught by the incident, including the coastal schooner *Alice S. Wentworth* whose bowsprit went into the after gangway and into the freight deck. The damage was slight and two tugs set both vessels free the next day. **Below:** Two months after the *Naushon* went aground, another island steamer, the *Nantucket*, went aground on the shoals at Sturgeon Flats after leaving Edgartown early in the morning. The vessel lay on the flats for seven days before she could be freed. *Photo from the collection of Paul C. Morris, Nantucket, Mass.*

The island steamer *Nantucket* aground on Sturgeon Flats in November, 1931. A dredge was brought in to dig a channel to free her. *Photo courtesy of Paul C. Morris, Nantucket, Mass.*

Above: On November 30, 1932, a barge was cast ashore in gale winds on Nantucket Island. The craft lost her rudder when she hit the beach but otherwise was in fair condition. She was later abandoned by her owners. Later, someone set her afire and the hull burned down to a small piece of wreckage which lay on the beach for years. *Photo courtesy of Charles F. Sayle, Nantucket, Mass.* **Below:** Another island steamer got into trouble on September 30, 1934. The *New Bedford* struck Weepecket Rock near Woods Hole and the ship was leaking so badly her Captain ran her ashore on nearby Uncatena Island. Her passengers were removed by local small craft. A few days later, with pumps working aboard the *New Bedford,* the tug *Resolute* pulled her free and towed her to dry-docks for repairs. *Photo from the collection of Paul C. Morris, Nantucket, Mass.*

Above: In the mid-1930's, work progressed on the widening and deepening of the Cape Cod Canal by the Federal Government. A mishap occurred to one of the dredges on January 27, 1937, when the *Governor Herrick* sprung a leak and sank while digging out a boulder from the bottom. The dredge was out of the channel and did not impede ship traffic. It was subsequently raised and repaired. *Photo courtesy of the Army Engineers, Cape Cod Canal.*
Below: The steamer *Canadian Planter* was in a collision with the steamer *City of Auckland,* late at night on May 3, 1936, in dense fog. The *Canadian Planter* sank on Horseshoe Shoal in Nantucket Sound. The crew from the *Planter* all went aboard the *City of Auckland.* The damaged freighter sank to her decks. The cargo was lost but the vessel was later salvaged. *Photo from the collection of Paul C. Morris, Nantucket, Mass.*

On May 6, 1937, the three masted schooner *Edward R. Smith* was in a collision with the Italian motor ship *Maria* about ten miles northeast of Provincetown. The mishap carried away the jibboom and headgear of the schooner. The steamer towed the *Smith* to Boston for repairs. *Photo courtesy of the Mariners Museum, Newport News, Virginia.*

On August 17, 1938, the U.S. Army engineers dredge *William T. Rossell* was working the Hog Island channel at midnight when she struck a rock on her starboard side. The accident tore a large hole in the side of the vessel and she sank on a shoal. A temporary patch was made and the ship raised. She was then towed to Boston for repairs. *Photo from the collection of Paul C. Morris, Nantucket, Mass.*

THE COAST PILOT BOOKS

In 1796, Edmund M. Blunt wrote the first "American Coast Pilot". It was privately published and was the beginning of a series. The book contained a variety of navigational information to assist the mariner in finding his way in and around the shoals and harbors along the coast. The publication was sold to the U.S. Coast Survey in 1867 and thereafter published by the U.S. Government. The U.S. Coast Pilot No. 1, Atlantic Coast, Eastport to Cape Cod contains information for navigators from the Cape north to Maine. The No. 2 book contains information from the Cape south to Sandy Hook in New Jersey. All small boats navigating these waters should have copies of the Coast Pilot aboard for the number one aid to navigation. There are ten books covering all of the coastlines of the United States including the East, West and Gulf coasts, the Great Lakes, Puerto Rico and the U.S. Virgin Islands, the Hawaiian Archipelago and the entire coast of Alaska.

The New England books contain a profusion of general information which includes data on Notices to Mariners, Customs Service, National Ocean Survey, Nautical Charts, tide tables, Coastal Current diagrams, Restricted areas, National Weather Service broadcasts, Storm warnings, Coast Guard Search and Rescue operations, Radio Distress procedures, Locations of Submarine cables and pipelines, obstructions to navigation, Aids to Navigation including lights, buoys, day beacons and fog signals, Radio beacons, clearance on bridges, use of Radar while underway and Navigation Regulations. These are but a few of the articles to interest the mariner. In addition, there are various tables pertaining to radio bearings, conversion tables for points of the compass, nautical to statute miles, tables of ocean distances between ports of the locations in the book, a table of Beaufort scale of wind force and climatological tables, all to aid the sailor to avoid the perils of shipwreck.

In 1932 the Government began to make improvements at the Cape Cod Canal. The waterway had been opened in 1915 under private ownership but large commercial vessels had difficulties while using the narrow canal. In 1928, the Federal Government purchased the canal. Between 1933 and 1935, two new highway bridges and a new railroad bridge were built. The canal was dredged to a width of 480 feet and a depth of 25 feet. A new lighthouse was built in 1941 on Cleveland Ledge in the middle of Buzzards Bay about seven miles southwest of the state pier.

The Nantucket Lightship station is fifty miles southeast of the island. It is the first glimpse of America to greet trans-Atlantic steamers. On May 15, 1934, the White Star liner *Olympic*, sister ship to the ill-fated *Titanic*, was steaming towards New York City in dense fog. She was guided by the radio beacon on the lightship which was picked up by her radio direction finder. Suddenly, as the huge liner loomed out of the fog, the lightship lay directly in her path. The crewmen aboard had no warning and the severed halves of the tiny vessel sank in less than a minute. Of the eleven men on board, seven were lost. The *Olympic* stopped and picked up four survivors and three bodies. The White Star Line commissioned the firm of Pusey and Jones of Wilmington, Delaware, to build a new ship to replace the one lost. This vessel remained on station from 1936 until 1973, when she was relieved by another lightship.

During January and February of 1936, a cold wave settled down over New England and the estuaries and bays froze up. Ice cakes piled up on each other and the Island steamers could not navigate to Nantucket. In Cape Cod Bay, one could see ice all the way to the horizon. The Coast Guard at this time were called on to carry out a rescue above and beyond the normal scope of their duty. On February 9th seven youths of the Civilian Conservation Corps Camp in Brewster went out on Cape Cod bay for a Sunday hike on the ice. The lads had been warned by their superiors not to venture out too far but boys in their late teens always seem to possess a far greater knowledge than their adult mentors. The group was five miles from shore when the tide changed. The ice moved and the boys floated away. The temperature dipped down to twenty degrees during the night and a large concentration of Coast Guard air, sea and land forces joined in a search for the stranded hikers. They were finally rescued by the Coast Guard cutter *Harriett Lane* in the middle of the bay after twenty hours on the ice. Three of the young men suffered from frost bite and they were all rushed to the hospital. The wind had shifted to the northwest and this prevented the ice floe from being carried out to sea. The cutter was able to maneuver close enough to launch a lifeboat and pick up the stranded youths. The young men all survived the ordeal and perhaps learned a lesson.

Above: The 5,135 ton freighter *Capillo* bound from Boston to New York City, ran aground on Shovelful Shoal off Monomoy Island on July 28, 1937. The Coast Guard Cutters *Faunce* and *Algonquin* rigged hawsers and pulled the ship clear. *Photo from the collection of Paul C. Morris, Nantucket, Mass.* **Below:** This photo appeared in the New Bedford Times on Thursday, March 23, 1939 with the following caption: "Captain Abbott Walker of Eastham, Captain Dan Gould of Orleans, and Captain Charles Keagan of Nauset Coast Guard Station are shown inspecting an ancient surfboat, discovered by Warren Edwards of Orleans and thought to be one used by the old Humane Society and probably buried for 70 years."

Above: The Boston trawler *Andover* went aground in the fog on December 10, 1938 on Nauset Beach in Chatham. The vessel had fifty thousand pounds of fish aboard but the surf finished her before she could be salvaged. **Below:** The last four masted schooner to be wrecked around Cape Cod was the *Laura Annie Barnes* from Lunenburg, Nova Scotia. During a snow squall on January 17, 1938, the large vessel grounded on Tuckernuck Shoal with a cargo of pulp wood bound for New Haven Connecticut. The Coast Guard attempted to pull the ship off the shoals but was not successful. A couple of subsequent storms broke up the vessel and she was a total loss. *Photo by Joseph Indio*

At 2 a.m. on December 10, 1938, the Boston beam trawler *Andover* went aground in fog on Nauset Beach in Orleans. Coast Guard Boatswain's Mate Bill Silva of the Orleans station heaved a line aboard her and the life- savers brought in seven crewmen using the breeches buoy. Two other crewmen launched a dory and came ashore. The rescue was directed by Chief Boatswain's Mate Alvin H. Wright. After coming ashore the Captain of the trawler said: "Our compass kind of let go and put us out of our reckoning. We got on the bar about a quarter past one, pounded over the bar and hit the beach. There was a heavy swell running. The Coast Guard did a wonderful job in the darkness as the waves were rolling completely over the vessel." The fishing boat was owned by the General Seafoods Corporation of Gloucester and was carrying a 50,000 pound catch after a week's fishing on Georges Bank. On December 13th a tugboat from the Merritt Chapman & Scott wrecking company arrived and put hawsers aboard to pull the vessel off but could not move her. Later heavy seas tossed the trawler high and dry on the beach and she was a total loss.

On January 17, 1939 the four masted schooner *Laura Annie Barnes* ran aground on Tuckernuck Shoal in Nantucket Sound. The vessel was built in 1921 at Phippsburg, Maine. She was of 698 gross tons and was 181 feet long. The ship had sailed out of Nova Scotia with a cargo of $10,000 worth of wood pulp in bales. Her owner and Captain was James L. Publicover of Dublin Shores, Nova Scotia. The Captain said that he ran into a northeast gale four days previous to stranding. The grounding occurred when his ship missed a tack. The vessel lay about four miles south of the Cross Rip Lightship. Captain Publicover added that his schooner had been a home to him and his three sons for the last twenty years. The schooner was in an excellent state of repair and one of the last of her kind sailing commercially on the east coast. Soon after the grounding, two Coast Guard cutters arrived to lend assistance but the vessel was hard on the shoal and could not be moved. The seas were making up and the waves were washing over the decks. In a short while the ship was in danger of breaking up. The Coast Guard removed the crew of seven men. The names of the crewmen were: William, Bruce and Charles Publicover, Fletcher Oxner, Wilbur Stevens and Arnold Adams. Another northeast storm on February 4th broke up the *Laura Annie Barnes* and it was a total loss.

On July 1, 1939, the U.S. Lighthouse Service was merged into the U.S. Coast Guard. The lightship crews, the men on the buoy tenders and ice breakers along with the lighthouse keepers were absorbed into the growing coastal service. The Lighthouse Service dated back to 1789. The keepers, were called "wickies" in the early days, because many of their daylight hours were spent cleaning the wicks. The light in the beacon was supplied by wicks burning whale oil. They carried on a variety of duties in addition to maintaining a light throughout the night and the foghorns in thick weather. Many of these persons, men and women, were decorated for heroism when they risked their lives in saving shipwrecked sailors near their stations. The lightships were the roughest duty in the service. The men lived in constant discomfort at sea and many lost their lives in storms and collisions. The civilians who stayed on in the Coast Guard have all been retired now. Most of the lighthouses are now deserted as modern electronics have replaced manpower. Automation is now the keeper of the lighthouses along our shores. The automation is monitored along the coast by personnel of the Coast Guard bases in the vicinity, to insure constant vigilance in the tradition of keeping the lights burning.

Above: The war exacted a heavy toll of lives and ships off the east coast during the early months of 1942. This unidentified vessel had been torpedoed and was burning. The losses in ships and men was heavy until the Navy was able to meet the threat of German U-boats and overcome it. **Below:** Clinging to a liferaft and tossing on stormy seas, sixteen survivors of a U.S. troop transport sunk by a Nazi U-boat were rescued by the U.S. Coast Guard Combat Cutter *Bibb*. The transport *Henry R. Mallory* was torpedoed with the loss of more than 300 American soldiers, sailors and marines. *Photos courtesy of the U.S. Coast Guard.*

The war in Europe escalated. France fell to Germany and England fought on doggedly with aid from the United States. As the country geared up for war production, merchant shipping increased. The accidents around Cape Cod continued. The Merchants & Miners vessel *Kent* ran up on the rocks between Gull and Penikese islands in Buzzards Bay. The ship grounded about 2 a.m. on March 12, 1941 and lay about two miles north of Cuttyhunk Island. The ship had on board a cargo of machinery and tools. She was bound from Boston to Norfolk, Virginia. Surfboats from the Cuttyhunk station went to the grounded freighter and carried hawsers to tugs. The *Kent* was to have been turned over to the Navy for conversion to a transport after discharging her cargo in Norfolk. Naval Intelligence officers arrived soon after to investigate rumors of sabotage. They interviewed the eighty-five members of the crew. On March 17th the cargo was removed and landed in New Bedford. On March 25th the salvage tug *Resolute* pulled the ship off the rocks and the next day she was towed to Boston for repairs.

In November 1941, President Roosevelt placed the operations of the Coast Guard under the jurisdiction of the U.S. Navy for the duration of the emergency. On December 7, 1941 the Empire of Japan attacked the United States. They bombed the U.S. fleet in Pearl Harbor, Hawaii and the country was drawn into World War II. Three days later the motor vessel *Oregon* was in collision with the battleship *New Mexico* 25 miles south of Nantucket Island. The collision occurred at night when both ships were observing wartime blackout and were running without lights. Seventeen men were lost from the *Oregon*. The Navy made no announcement about damage or casualties aboard the battleship. Some of the survivors were brought ashore by the New Bedford fishing trawler *Viking*.

The German U-boats began to take a terrible toll of American merchant shipping just off our shores. In January 1942 they sank 23 ships. More in February when the score was 30. Thirty more were sunk in March, 38 in April, 44 in May and 55 in June. The mute evidence washed ashore. Oil soaked bodies were discovered by the beach patrols. Most of this activity took place off the shores of Cape Hatteras in North Carolina. Off Cape Cod there were several incidents rumored but never reported in the local press. This carnage continued until the Coast Guard and Navy units went to war on the submarines in the Western Atlantic. The British freighter *Peisander* was torpedoed and sunk by the German submarine U-653 about seven hundred miles southeast of Nantucket Island on May 17, 1942. Three lifeboats were launched by the 61 man crew from the sinking ship. Five days later, two boats with 43 survivors were discovered on the shoals by the Coast Guard from the Madaket station at Nantucket. They were quickly brought ashore. A Navy plane sighted the other boat and the cutter *General Greene* was dispatched to pick them up. There was dense fog in the area around the Nantucket shoals but the cutter found them on May 25th. A submarine was spotted nearby and the cutter attacked with depth charges. There was a large oil slick after the battle. The *General Greene* stopped to pick up the men from the lifeboat. The survivors said that the U-boat had been following them ever since their ship had been sunk. The sub had torpedoed the U.S. freighter *Plow City* when that vessel had tried to rescue them.

In order to supplement their forces, the Coast Guard Auxiliary act was amended in 1942. Yachtsmen and pilots all joined to assist in the war effort. They formed a "Ghost Fleet" to patrol off shore in search of enemy U-boats. By December, 1942, the Coast Guard had acquired over two thousand boats, most of which became coastal pickets sailing under the logo of the Corsair Fleet. They carried out patrols and rescue work. The larger sailing vessels were invaluable in submarine patrol because of their stealth. They were built to sail in stormy weather at sea and were equipped with two way radios for communications. These boats worked with the air arm of the Navy. If an enemy was sighted, planes were dispatched to the scene. The patrols were usually tedious and hazardous. There were many long fruitless days and nights at sea in all kinds of weather.

At the outbreak of war, beach patrols were instituted along the entire coastlines of the U.S. On June 13, 1942, four German saboteurs landed on the beach at Amagansett, Long Island in New York. They were intercepted by Seaman second class John C. Cullen on his normal nightly beach patrol. Cullen accepted some money from the men to let the Germans think he would not report them. He hurried back to the station and alerted other crewmen. An armed group of Coast Guards returned to the location but the Germans had disappeared. Later officials found high explosives, detonators and other devices buried in the sand. The FBI apprehended the saboteurs shortly thereafter but on June 17th four more men were landed from a U-boat at Ponte Vedra Beach in Florida. These men too, were arrested by the FBI and the the need for security along the

Above: The *Cassiar*, a 64-foot sport fisherman yacht was employed during wartime as a member of the "Corsair Fleet" operating around Cape Cod. The boat was owned by Mr. Richard K. Mellon. These small auxiliary vessels helped the Coast Guard during the entire war. **Below:** On June 2, 1942, the *H.M.S. Mattawin* was torpedoed by a German submarine 200 miles east of Cape Cod. Some of the crew managed to make it to a lifeboat and the survivors came ashore on the beach at Eastham, south of the Coast Guard Station. The crewmen were taken to the station and the boat sanded in on the beach. A storm later broke up the remains of the lifeboat. *Photo courtesy of Helen Schwind, Eastham, Mass.*

shoreline was evident. Armed beach patrols were established as a supplement to port security. The original Life Saving Service had patrolled the beaches as part of their operations to watch for shipwrecks and to save lives. The war patrols were set up somewhat differently. It was primarily as a security force to protect the shores against landings by saboteurs, communications between people on shore and the enemy at sea, enemy landings, fifth column activities and to guard against intrusion in restricted areas. No enemy landings were known to have occurred on Cape Cod during the war. A directive issued by headquarters outlined the duties of the beach patrol: "These beach patrols are not intended as a military protection of our coastline, as this is the function of the Army. The beach patrols are more in the nature of outposts to report activities along the coastline and are not to repel hostile armed units. The function of the Army in this connection is not to guard against surreptitious acts, but rather to furnish the armed forces required to resist any attempt by armed enemy forces or parties to penetrate the coastline by force."

In 1942, the Coast Guard set up the "Temporary Reserves". These were volunteers who served on a part time basis. The minimum was twelve hours a week without pay. By June, 1944 it was estimated that over fifty thousand volunteers were serving and they released over eight thousand full time Coast Guard men for other vital duties at sea. The Temporary Reserves aided in all phases of port security. The chain of Coast Guard lifeboat stations, lighthouses and lookout stations provided the bases for the coast watch. Several new stations were built in addition to hundreds of lookout towers. The use of two-way radio and telephones enabled coast watchers to pass along information on vessels in distress, aircraft crashes, landings, flashing lights, flares, fires, unidentified aircraft or ships, gunfire, explosions, mines and wreckage ashore.

On Cape Cod, the men and women were engaged in communications, harbor patrols, guard details, off-shore coastal pickets and beach patrols. The beach patrols were the first arm of our national defense. The entire coastline of the United States was patrolled except for inaccessible areas. The men carried out their patrols on foot, in jeeps, on horseback and aboard boats along the Atlantic, Gulf and Pacific coasts. There were no horse patrols in the first district which included Cape Cod. In areas where there was a danger of invasion, a 24 hour patrol was maintained. In other areas only night patrols were carried on except in thick weather. Lookouts, however, were continuous around the clock. The two man patrols were later reduced to only one man when the guard dogs were employed. The type of dog generally used was the German Shepherd. The patrolmen found flotsam and jetsam, mines, bombs, booby traps and wreckage. They assisted in life saving of persons from downed aircraft and wrecked vessels. They also sent help to small boats in trouble off shore. The danger of enemy landings declined in the summer of 1943 and the patrols were reduced. They were again diminished in April of 1944 and were stopped when the war ended. On September 2, 1945, ceremonies of surrender were conducted aboard the Battleship Missouri in Tokyo Bay and an uneasy peace settled over the world.

On the morning of April 25, 1945, Cape Codders witnessed a large liberty ship being towed by Navy tugs into Cape Cod Bay. The vessel was grounded on a shoal off Eastham and has never moved since that day. The ship was the *SS James Longstreet.* She was destined to become a training target for bombs, rockets and missiles fired at it by the various military air forces in the New England sector. The ship was bombarded for thirty years until local protests succeeded in stopping the practice. To be able to withstand all of the explosions and unknown ordinance dropped on it and still stand out of water is a tribute to the durability of American ships built during the war. At this writing, however, the midships area has fallen in on itself and the remainder of the hull resembles swiss cheese.

Early Sunday morning, August 25, 1940, the Newport trawler *Palestine* came ashore on Long Nook beach in Truro. The cause of the grounding was blamed on a faulty compass. Coast Guardsmen worked for two days and with the aid of the cutters *Harriet Lane* and *Travis* pulled the vessel off into deep water. The grounding brought hundreds out to view the event and two artists recorded the scene on canvas.

Above: On October 27, 1943, the cargo ship *James Longstreet* was driven ashore on Sandy Hook, New Jersey. The grounding broke the back of the ship and she was never again to sail under her own power. The Navy used her as a target ship for various experiments until April, 1945, when they towed it into Cape Cod Bay and grounded on a shoal a mile off Eastham. The numerous military units around southern New England used the derelict as a target for bombs, rockets and guns for thirty years until today the hull is fallen in on itself amidships.*Photo by Burke Maloney, Asbury Park Press.* **Below:** The vessel today has deteriorated to the point where only the bow and stern are left above water. Time and erosion will ultimately consume the remnants of the ship *James Longstreet. Aerial Photo by the Author.*

On September 14, 1944, another hurricane hit southeastern New England. The 100 mile-per-hour winds destroyed homes, toppled trees and caused one hundred million dollars in property damage from Rhode Island to Provincetown. Because of adequate warnings by radio, only 31 deaths were recorded. Twelve of these were the crew of the Vineyard Lightship which went down with all hands during the storm. Mr. Harold W. Flagg of Sagamore Village in the town of Bourne was a crew member of the lightship on shore leave at the time of the tragedy and remembered the ship, her record and the crewmen lost.

1901 VINEYARD SOUND LIGHTSHIP 1944

The VINEYARD SOUND LIGHTSHIP was built by the Spedden Ship Building Co., of Baltimore, Maryland in 1901 and was designated No. 73. The early years of the "73" were spent on Pollock Rip, Cape Cod, Mass. Later the ship was transferred to the Sow and Pigs reef at the western end of Cuttyhunk Island and given the name "VINEYARD." Many ships have come to grief in this area, as did the famous New Bedford whaler *Wanderer* in August of 1924.

In these same waters, the VINEYARD, faithful guardian of all shipping, for over forty years, came to her own tragic end. It was during the early hours of September 14, 1944, while in the throes of a violent hurricane that this well known beacon and the lives of the entire on board crew were extinguished for all time. A few days later the ship was located, settled upright but completely dismasted in sixty feet of water, having dragged anchor more than a mile from her designated station.

The following named men were on board and lost with the ship:

SEVIGNY, Edgar CAPT.	Boatswain, U.S.C.G.
STECKLING, Edward	Chief M.M., U.S.C.G.
KOLOSKY, John	M.M. 2/c, U.S.C.G.R.
TALBOT, Richard R.	Ships Cook 2/c, U.S.C.G.R.
STARRATT, Lawrence R.	M.M. 3/c, U.S.C.G.R.
STELTER, Frederick J.	Watertender 3/c, U.S.C.G.R.
MICHALAK, Peter P.	Seaman 1/c, U.S.C.G.R.
STIMAC, John J.	Seaman 1/c, U.S.C.G.R.
HAMMETT, Jack M.	Seaman 1/c, U.S.C.G.
GORDON, J.G.	Seaman 1/c, U.S.C.G.R.
HULL, Allen L.	Seaman 2/c, U.S.C.G.R.
CONSTANTINE, Vangal	Seaman 2/c, U.S.C.G.R.

The September, 1944 hurricane sank the Vineyard Lightship with her twelve man crew. The above photo is a side scan sonar print of the wreckage on the bottom in Buzzards Bay. The bow is to the left and the stern to the right. Amidships are shadows of the mast, base of the stack and bulkhead beams. *Photo courtesy of Arnold Carr.*

On Friday, January 3, 1947, at 8 a.m. the Madaket Coast Guard Station on the west coast of Nantucket was closed in an economy move. The station was not considered necessary. The personnel were transferred to the Brant Point station at the entrance to Nantucket harbor. Late that afternoon, the 339 foot Panamanian freighter *Kotor* ran aground in dense fog, two miles east of the newly closed Madaket Station. The ship was stranded just a short distance from the western tip of the island. The *Kotor* was of 3,678 tons bound from New York City to Halifax, Nova Scotia with a mixed cargo and Austrailian wool. She was in no immediate danger. Miss Mildred Jewett, a resident of Madaket saw the lights of the vessel and went to the beach. She called the Coast Guard at about five o'clock in the afternoon to report the grounding. Miss Jewett was a regular beachcomber and often reported to the Coast Guard about the accidents at that end of the island. She came to be known as "Madaket Millie". A Coast Guard crew arrived shortly and launched a dory under the direction of Chief Boatswain's Mate Frank Masaschi. They rowed out to the *Kotor* to check on the conditions aboard. The next afternoon two cutters from Woods Hole pulled the ship off the shoal and she was towed to Newport, Rhode Island.

Above: The Boston fishing schooner *Mary E. O'Hara* returning from the fishing grounds at night struck an unlighted anchored barge and sunk in January, 1944. The temperature was about ten degrees and the crew froze to death in the rigging before they discovered after daylight. A Coast Guard 36-foot motor lifeboat inspected the wreck, with her masts rising out of the depths. *Photo courtesy of Charles F. Sayle, Nantucket, Mass.* **Below:** On September 14, 1944, a hurricane hit southeastern New England. Property damage was heavy all along the coastline. The Woods Hole Oceanographic Institute's ketch *Atlantis* was blown ashore at Penzance Point in Woods Hole. The picturesque vessel was later refloated. *Photo courtesy of the Woods Hole Oceanographic Institute, Woods Hole, Massachusetts.*

Above: The Gloucester dragger *Donald and Johnny* ran aground on Nauset Beach, one mile below the Orleans Coast Guard station in a heavy fog on July 22, 1946. The vessel had a cargo of ten thousand pounds of fish in the hold. The Coast Guard removed the crew but the dragger and cargo were a total loss. *Photo by True Fife, Eastham, Mass.*
Below: The Panamanian freighter *Kotor* ran aground in dense fog off the western end of Nantucket Island on January 2, 1947. The Coast Guard station at Madaket had just been decommissioned that morning as an economy move by the Coast Guard and all personnel had been transferred to the other end of the island. Three Coast Guard cutters pulled the ship off a couple of days later and towed her to New York City. *Photo courtesy of Charles F. Sayle, Nantucket, Mass.*

After the war there were twelve German U-boats in the custody of the United States Government. One was deeded to the Museum of Science and Industry in Chicago and is still on display there. Three were sold for scrap metal and the remainder were sunk testing torpedoes. This is the U-234, sunk on November 20, 1947 forty miles northeast of Cape Cod. She went down in 600 feet of water after being sunk by the U.S.S. Greenfish. *Photo from the National Archives, Washington, D.C.*

Chapter Eight

After World War II the Coast Guard stations along the backside of Cape Cod were abandoned one by one and closed down. The introduction of modern aircraft into search and rescue, along with amphibious vehicles, enabled fewer men to cover wider areas of this treacherous coastline. Two stations, from the original thirteen along the outer shore were left manned and ready. The Race Point in Provincetown and the Chatham station which, along with the Brant Point in Nantucket and the Menemsha on Martha's Vineyard, the Woods Hole and Cape Cod Canal stations completed the coverage for the Cape area.

Another succession of tragedies occured along the shores of Cape Cod in the 1950's. On the night of April 7, 1950, a howling northeast storm with seventy m.p.h. winds was lashing the outer Cape. The fishing vessel *William J. Landry* was working in from Georges Bank and leaking very badly. Her Captain had radioed the Coast Guard for assistance but before any could arrive the small Fairhaven vessel sank with her crew of eight men, three of whom came from Nantucket. Another vessel, the Gloucester dragger *Four Sisters* with a crew of ten disappeared in the same storm without a trace. Another storm with gale force winds drove the Gloucester dragger *Mary M.* aground off Cuttyhunk island on November 27, 1951. The 85' vessel had grounded twice near the west end of the island when she hit a rock and broke up in heavy surf. Five men were lost in the accident. Only one man survived. He was William H. Sheppard of New Bedford. Mr. Sheppard swam a short distance through boiling surf to West Beach where he alerted the Coast Guard by telephone about the disaster. They searched the area with boats and a helicopter but failed to turn up any trace of the missing men. Only one body was found.

On January 30, 1952, off Provincetown, six crewmen from the 80' trawler *Marie & Winifred* were saved by the Coast Guard during a northeast snowstorm after the vessel had grounded on a shoal. Boats on the fishing vessel had been smashed by towering waves during the storm. Chief Boatswain's mate Don Corea and his crewmen; BM1 Don Heath and Eng.3 Warren Quinn* manned the 36' motor lifeboat from the Race Point station after the *Marie & Winifred* had radioed for help. Six men were rescued off the flooded vessel just in time. The fishing vessel was later towed in to Provincetown Harbor by the Coast Guard.

One of the most spectacular rescues on the east coast of the United States was made on the night of February 18, 1952, when two tankers broke in half off Cape Cod during a fierce northeaster. In sixty foot waves, a crew of four men in a 36' motor lifeboat from the Chatham Coast Guard station, rescued thirty-two men off the stern half of the tanker *Pendleton* and brought them back to shore. The four crewmen, Coxswain Bernard C. Webber, Engineer Andrew J. Fitzgerald and seamen Richard P. Livesey and Irving W. Maske were all awarded the Gold Lifesaving Medal for their valor and bravery during the most difficult rescue. The medal is considered to be on a parallel with the Congressional Medal of Honor. The tanker had broken in two off Provincetown and the pieces of the vessel had drifted down the backside of Cape Cod during the day. When the derelict was discovered, late in the afternoon, Webber and his crew were dispatched to save the men off the stern half of the tanker. The *Fort Mercer* broke in half in heavy seas thirty miles off the backside of Cape Cod. Other units of the Coast Guard were working the rescue of the tanker off shore. A total of 14 men were lost from the two vessels in the storm but seventy were saved.

*Warren Quinn is the Author's brother.

An artists conception of the stormy conditions off Chatham on the night of February 18, 1952, when the Coast Guard lifeboat CG 36500 rescued 32 men, off the broken stern of the *S.S. Pendleton* during a raging northeast storm.

Above: The stern section of the ship after it grounded about one mile off Monomoy Island, south of Chatham. *Official U.S. Coast Guard Photograph.* **Below:** The blizzard of 1978 toppled the wreckage of the *Pendleton* and it was declared unsafe for small craft in the area. A contractor was hired and the remains were dynamited to reduce the level of wreckage. This enabled small craft to navigate the area. *Aerial photo by the Author.*

Above: On October 30, 1950, the Chatham fishing vessel *Cachalot* was returning from a fishing trip and was hit by a big wave while coming over Chatham Bar. The vessel pitchpoled and two crewmen were drowned. Later a crew of men tried to turn the boat over as the "CG 36500", the motor lifeboat from the Chatham station pulled on her with a line. *Photo from a souvenir postcard.* **Below:** After World War II, the Coast Guard utilized new equipment developed during the war. One unique vehicle was the DUKW, an amphibious vessel. The one pictured was attached to the Race Point Station. Most all stations on the Cape had the amphibians to facilitate a quick rescue off the beach. The vessel handled quite badly in rough weather and was only used when conditions permitted. *Photo by Gordon C. Caldwell, Hyannis, Mass.*

On June 20, 1952 the Gloucester fishing vessel *Albatross* was in collision with the 10,000 ton tanker *Esso Chattanooga* three miles off Highland Light at 2:30 a.m. in heavy seas. The crew of the smaller vessel launched a dory and, with twelve men aboard, Captain Ejorgvin Einarsson gave his life for his shipmates when he refused to overload the boat. The survivors were picked up by the tanker and brought to Boston. The Captain of the tanker, Thomas B. Cristiansen told Coast Guard officials that he looked for several hours but could not find a trace of Captain Einarsson. Another collision occurred on October 4, 1954, near the Nantucket lightship when the French freighter *Tofevo* was rammed by the 15,000 ton Holland-America liner *Maasdam*. The liner was bound for Europe with 523 passengers, none of whom was injured. Damage was heavy to the bow of the liner. When the ships reached New York, passengers were furious when the Holland-America line refused to pay for passage aboard other liners leaving for Europe. The *Maasdam* was an economy liner and the delays caused inconveniences for her passengers. Several were offered and accepted passage on sister ships of the same line, leaving a few days later.

A snowstorm on November 20, 1955, with 80 m.p.h. wind gusts and high seas drove the 72' New Bedford fishing vessel *Abram H.* aground at the entrance to Nantucket harbor. An amphibious DUKW removed the ten member crew safely and landed them ashore. The *Abram H.* was later pulled off and refloated. In Plymouth Harbor the forty foot schooner *Snow Maiden* went aground on a sand bar. The Coast Guard rescued four men and two others came ashore in a dory. Off shore the Coast Guard were engaged in several rescues. The fishing vessel *M.C. Ballard* reported that she was taking on water off Georges Bank and waiting Coast Guard assistance. A small boat was missing in the vicinity of Cuttyhunk with two men aboard from Westport. Two other vessels were under tow to port by the Coast Guard. The *Catherine T.* with a seven man crew had been adrift for two days. The *Midway* had a broken rudder 27 miles southeast of the Pollock Rip Lightship and was being assisted by the Coast Guard cutter *Hornbeam*. In the meantime, one hundred miles off the backside of Cape Cod, the Liberian freighter *Daytona*, a converted LST, with a crew of 24 men had radioed for help. The vessel had suffered storm damage and had developed a starboard list. A search for the 322-foot ship proved fruitless. Wreckage was spotted a few days later and the she was presumed to be lost with all hands.

Late in the evening of July 25, 1956, the Italian liner *Andrea Doria* collided with the Swedish motor ship *Stockholm* fifty miles south of Nantucket Island in dense fog. It was just after eleven at night and the SOS brought scores of ships to the scene. The rescue effort saved 1662 persons off the ill-fated liner. Fifty-two had been killed in the initial collision. On the following day, the *Andrea Doria* sank in 225 feet of water. The modern liners rely on their radar during fog to hold their speed and maintain schedules. Cause of the accident was attributed to careless and negligent operation of the electronic eye and the evasion tactics employed prior to the collision. It was observed later that if the ships had not been equipped with radar the accident might have been avoided. The death toll on this famous wreck keeps rising. Divers continue to go down to the *Andrea Doria* each year in search of souvenirs. The ship is more than two hundred feet deep with strong ocean currents and cold water. It is a dive recommended for the more experienced and stronger divers. Joseph M. Drozd, 42, of Stonington, Connecticut died on July 14, 1988 while diving in the Ambrose Shipping Lanes, 46 miles south of Nantucket Island on the wreck. The fatality was the third diving victim, since the ship sank in 1956.

The Texas Tower No. 2, Georges Bank Station lay one hundred miles due east of Chatham, Massachusetts. The base was serviced by helicopters from Otis Air Force Base in Falmouth. Supplies, mail and personnel were carried out on a regular schedule.. The three lines hanging down from the center of the tower were to reverse the electrolysis of the sea water on the three legs by continually coating metal on the surfaces as fast as it was eaten off by the ocean. *Photo by the Author.*

THE TEXAS TOWERS - RADAR ISLANDS IN THE ATLANTIC

In April, 1955, the government announced plans to build a chain of radar islands extending 1,500 miles along the Atlantic coast from Norfolk, Virginia to Newfoundland and to be manned by the U.S. Air Force. The concept was a protective measure to avoid any sneak attack and was part of the continental Air Defense System of the United States. The raised platforms were called Texas Towers after the oil rigs in the Gulf of Mexico. They were six-thousand ton triangular platforms measuring 200 feet on each side. The stations were built in a shipyard and launched into the water. They were towed by tug-boats to the off-shore sites, and raised on several temporary caissons until the permanent legs were buried in the ocean bed. A chain of thirty stations was planned. The Georges Bank tower was the first erected, one-hundred miles due east of Chatham.

The off-shore bases were designed to be self sustaining and housed between fifty and seventy-five men. Beside the operational spaces, the station contained living quarters, a sick bay, maintenance facilities and recreation rooms. Part of the top deck was used as a helicopter landing pad. There were three large domes on one side of the tower which housed the radar. Located on the shore end of the platform were the tropo scatter communication dishes. The Georges Bank tower was towed in place on July 14, 1955. A month later the platform had been raised on her temporary legs when hurricane Connie blew up from the Caribbean. The storm passed without any damage and the workers labored to finish the ten million dollar project. Another storm in November damaged the fenders on the permanent legs. They were removed and not replaced. On December 8, 1955 the base was completed and turned over to the Air Force and operations began.

The dredge NAHANT of the New England Dredge & Dock company burned almost to the waterline early in the morning of March 26, 1952. The vessel was tied up to the west mooring basin at the Cape Cod Canal and was a complete loss. *Photos courtesy of the Corps of Engineers.*

A second station was launched in August of 1956 and towed to a location twenty-seven miles south of Nantucket Island. The third station was launched and positioned 80 miles off the coast of New Jersey. On the night of January 15, 1961, the New Jersey station collapsed into the Atlantic killing 28 airmen and civilian construction workers on board. The Georges Shoal and Nantucket towers were located on the shoals in less than 70 feet of water. The New Jersey tower was located in 185 feet of water and was unstable. It had acquired the nickname of "Old Shaky". U.S. Senate investigators blamed the loss of the tower on the designers and building contractors. Further blame was laid on the Navy and Air Force who supervised the installation.

On April 23, 1962, two fishermen were saved by the quick action of four airmen on board the tower off Nantucket. The 54 foot dragger *Nelly* was fishing four miles south of the station in high winds and six foot seas when she suddenly developed a leak. The water could not be controlled and the boat sank taking one man down with her. The other two crewmen, Earl O. Andrews of New Bedford, Captain of the vessel and Wilson McDonald of Fairhaven were rescued by a motorized longboat which had been launched from the Nantucket Shoals tower. The boat was manned by Staff Sergeant William B. Hartwell of San Antonio, Texas; Arthur T. Williams of Altoona, Pa., Robert Caranci of Plymouth, Massachusetts, and Airman 2C Gary Blemaster of Harper Woods, Michigan. The boat was one of two kept aboard the station ready for launching. The water was very cold and the men could not have survived very long because of hypothermia. Both men were wearing life jackets and were near the point of passing out when they were picked up by the airmen. They were brought to the tower and treated for exposure, then flown by helicopter to Otis Air Force Base.

In May, 1962, the Texas Towers were declared obsolete by the Air Force. Bids were let for demolition of the two remaining towers. The pounding of the sea and the rusting of the legs was given as a reason for their destruction. Radar picket planes flying in relays over the Atlantic, equipped with newer long range automatic radar, replaced the platforms in the ocean. The tower on Georges Bank was blasted off her permanent legs in September, 1963. On October 1st, while being towed into port to be cut up for scrap, the tower sank in rough seas 150 miles east of Provincetown and was lost. With the bad news overshadowing the good, it isn't any wonder that no one thought of making an off-shore rescue station out of the Georges Bank tower. Rescue helicopters today have to fly a hundred miles to the scene when a fishing boat gets in trouble on the banks.

Above: The *Santina D.,* a fishing vessel aground near Race Point in Provincetown. The fuel vessel *Neptune* is tied alongside. This was another grounding in the long list of mishaps to the Provincetown fishing fleet. *Photo by Neal Nickerson, Provincetown, Mass.* **Below:** Another unidentified fishing trawler ashore and wrecked in the pounding surf. Salvage at this point was impossible. *Photo courtesy of Harold B. Jennings, Eastham, Mass.*

Above: On August 31, 1954, hurricane Carol lashed Cape Cod with high winds and storm surge tides. At Woods Hole, the parking lot was flooded by the high tide. The motor vessel *Islander* was tossed around in her berth and was in danger of being heavily damaged. Captain Alec Smith got underway and found a lee cove on Martha's Vineyard. He rode out the storm and saved his vessel. **Below:** At Dyers dock in Woods Hole a schooner and cabin cruiser were both sunk during the storm on August 31, 1954. *Photos by S. J. Turner*

Above: Late at night on July 25, 1956, about fifty miles south of Nantucket Island, the Swedish motor vessel *Stockholm* collided with the Italian liner *Andrea Doria* in dense fog. This photograph was made at about nine a.m. the following morning looking down on the decks off the starboard bow. Notice the lifeboats on the port side still in their davits. The crew were unable to lower these boats because of the steep starboard list following the collision. **Below:** The luxury liner took her final dive to the bottom of the ocean. The photograph was made from a Coast Guard amphibian at the moment the stern was disappearing from the surface of the ocean. *Photos courtesy of the U.S. Coast Guard.*

The *Stockholm* limped into New York harbor on July 27, 1956. A helicopter hovered close to survey the damage. The anchors of the vessel were locked on the bottom of the ocean following the collision and the chains had to be cut to free the liner. It took two days to reach New York. The rescue of 1,662 passengers and crew from the *Andrea Doria* was carried out by Coast Guard, Navy and merchant vessels that answered the S.O.S. *Photo courtesy of the U.S. Coast Guard.*

Above: The New Bedford scallop dragger *Abram H* ran aground at the entrance to Nantucket harbor during a snowstorm on November 20, 1955. The crew of ten was saved by the Coast Guard. The fishing vessel was hauled off the beach a few days later by Coast Guard cutters. *Photo courtesy of Charles F. Sayle, Nantucket, Mass.* **Below:** The collier *Reading,* loaded with ten thousand tons of coal ran onto Henrietta Rock in Buzzards Bay on February 18, 1957. The rock cracked the hull and the vessel was impaled on the reef until she was unloaded by salvage crews. *Photo by the author.*

An L.N.B. (Large navigational buoy) was placed on the Nantucket Lightship station on August 10, 1982, near the lightship to ascertain if the structure could take the punishing conditions at the station, fifty miles southeast of Nantucket Island. The experiment worked well and on July 21, 1983, the Nantucket Lightship departed her station. Thus ended 159 years of continuous service by lightships of the United States. The Nantucket Lightship was the last of her type on duty in U.S. waters. *Photograph by Gordon E. Caldwell, Hyannis, Mass.*

As years passed, manned lightships became more expensive to operate. There were six remaining around Cape Cod in the 1950's. These were later replaced with buoys over a period of twenty years. The Handkerchief was retired in 1951. Next was the Hens and Chickens in 1954. In 1961, the Vineyard Lightship was replaced by a large four legged steel tower. The tower has living quarters on the lower deck and a helicopter landing pad on the top deck. In 1963 the Stonehorse Lightship was replaced by a fixed beacon. This left only two vessels. The vessel at Cross Rip was withdrawn in 1964 and the final retirement was at Pollock Rip in 1969. The last lightship on active duty in the United States was the Nantucket. On August 10, 1982 an L.N.B. (Large Navigational Buoy) was placed on the Nantucket station alongside the lightship as a test to ascertain if the buoy could withstand the punishing weather and hold station. The experiment proved successful and on July 21, 1983 the Nantucket lightship departed her station for the last time after 130 years of continuous service to the ships at sea.

Weather
Scattered showers tonight, low in low 50s. Fair Thursday, colder.

Cape Cod Standard-Times

Final Edition

World Dispatches From Leased Wires

"Forward With Cape Cod"

All the Local and State News

VOL. 24, NO. 237 — Fourteen Pages — HYANNIS, MASSACHUSETTS, WEDNESDAY, NOVEMBER 16, 1960 — FIVE CENTS — In combination with The New Bedford Standard-Times SEVEN CENTS

452-Foot Freighter Aground At Southwest End of Canal

Ballot Law Criticized By Cape Town Clerks

The new State law prohibiting the counting of ballots until after the close of polling places brought almost unanimous disapproval from town clerks of Cape Cod's 15 communities. The law, passed by the State Legislature last Spring, was in effect for the first time in the presidential primaries in September.

Response from the town officials ranged from outright condemnation to dubious acceptance of the law which, in every town, extended the ballot counting time by several hours and increased election costs.

Machines Favored

In nearly every instance town clerks said they favored the purchase of voting machines, but ruled out the machines as impractical and an unnecessary expense if the current election law is repealed.

All the officials questioned deplored the enactment of the law which, they said, did nothing to facilitate the counting of votes and actually hampered the count because of the mental strain and fatigue it caused election workers.

Barnstable Town Clerk Howard W. Sears expressed his disapproval of the law as it is now set up.

"We have always stayed until the ballots were counted. The disadvantage now is that we get the results at a much later hour and at more expense to the town."

Cost Emphasized

Mr. Sears said that under the present law he favored the use of voting machines, although their cost — $1,700 each — was considerable.

"The State advises us that we would need a machine for every 400 voters. That would mean 20 machines for our nearly 8,000 registered voters or a cost to the town of $34,000," he said.

Mr. Sears said the only way to get the law repealed would be from public pressure on legislators.

Gerald Cash, Yarmouth town clerk, felt the new requirements had both beneficial and detrimental effects.

Unit Favors Law

"The State Town Clerks Association has gone on record as favoring the law because it prevents election trends from leaking out to the public and thus possibly influencing late voters."

He said many clerks are fighting the law because it forced them

Cape Hospital Elects Payson

Starts 6th Term As President

HYANNIS, Nov. 16—Randolph Payson of Hyannis Port, who has served as president of the Cape Cod Hospital for the last five years, was re-elected yesterday at the annual meeting of the hospital's board of directors. His sixth term is for one year.

Meeting at the hospital, the board of trustees also re-elected as vice-presidents Mrs. John E. Hinckley of Hyannis and Ralph B. Snow of Harwich Port. A new vice-president elected was Fred M. Rowell of Osterville.

Walcott Ames and Clarence W. Wyatt of Osterville were re-elected as auditors for the board.

Five Re-elected

Five persons were re-elected to the executive committee. They are Oscar Cahoon, Mrs. David M. Davis, and Mr. Snow of Harwich Port, Urban S. Livingston of Orleans and Robert Swan of Hyannis Port.

The corporation elected Mrs. Norman S. Everett of Barnstable its clerk, Edward W. Gould Jr. of Barnstable its treasurer and Hyman N. Hirsch of Hyannis as assistant treasurer.

The entire slate of 10 trustees was renamed for three year terms. Elected to serve one year to fill vacancies were Robert H. Morrison of West Yarmouth and Judge Henry L. Murphy of Centerville.

New members elected to serve for one year are C. Lee Austin of Barnstable, Robert Frothingham of Osterville, James Coggeshall of Barnstable and John T. Manning 3d of Chatham. There are 60 persons who are serving for one-year terms.

Reports were heard from Dr. Earle H. Webster, chief of staff,

Kennedy Shifts Holiday Plans

Will Forego Visit To Hyannis Port

By United Press International

PALM BEACH, Fla., Nov. 16—Before departing for a meeting in Texas with Senator Johnson, President-elect Kennedy today arranged to extend his stay in Florida.

Instead of following an original plan for spending Thanksgiving at his home on Cape Cod, Kennedy announced he will spend the holiday in Washington with his wife and young daughter. Then he will return to Florida.

Kennedy planned to take off today for Austin, Texas, in a chartered jet for an overnight stay at the ranch of his running-mate. He will return to Florida tomorrow night.

Don Wilson, acting press secretary to the President-elect said Kennedy on next Wednesday would fly to Washington and spend Thanksgiving with his wife, Jacqueline, and their daughter, Caroline, who will be 3 years old Nov. 27.

Kennedy planned to fly back to Florida Thanksgiving night or the following morning, and remain here for another five or six days.

Mrs. Kennedy is expecting her second child early next month and Wilson explained the decision to have the family Thanksgiving in Washington instead of Hyannis Port was because such an arrangement would be more convenient for her.

Kennedy apparently is returning to Florida after Thanksgiving because he feels the need for more rest from the rigors of his election campaign.

(Staff Photo by Gordon E. Caldwell)

The 452-foot American Export Company freighter SS Exermont went aground at about 6 this morning near Bassett Point in Gray Gables near the western end of the land cut of the Cape Cod Canal. Most canal traffic was halted at 7 a.m. The vessel, aground near the Summer White House of former President Grover Cleveland, was taking on water. Early attempts to free the vessel failed.

Ship Damaged In Accident

Freeing Attempt Set for Tonight

By DAVID MANNING
Cape Cod Standard-Times Staff Writer

BUZZARDS BAY, Nov. 16—The 6,675 ton American Export Line freighter SS Exermont went aground about 6 this morning in dense fog between Beacon 18 and Buoy 16 approximately 150 feet off Bassett Point on the southwestern end of the Cape Cod Canal.

The 452-foot vessel, bound from Boston to Norfolk, Va. slipped through the canal past the U.S. Army Corps of Engineers administration building at 5:45 a.m. and was advised by canal patrolmen to move along a bit faster due to the heavy fog rolling in. The visibility at the office building at that time was about a half mile.

Dispatcher William Chase, upon noticing the ship had gone aground, dispatched a patrol craft to the stricken vessel and called out the canal emergency crews.

Canal Closed

The waterway was closed to most traffic at 7 a.m. by Harold Gamble, engineer-in-charge.

The first disaster call was logged by radio operators at the U. S. Coast Guard Search and Rescue Communications Center in Boston at 7:09 a.m. Lieutenant Francis Flynn said the message notified authorities the vessel was aground and that it requested immediate assistance.

Shortly before 10 a.m. a radio message to the Coast Guard from the Exermont was relayed to the engineers indicating the vessel was shipping water in the 3, 4 and

'First Landing' Pageant Set

Scouts to Join In Cape-tip Event

PROVINCETOWN, Nov. 16—Annual re-enactment of the First Landing of the Pilgrims in

Regional School Unit Approves 1961 Budget

Senate Choice Is Discussed

Furcolo to Weigh Kennedy Selection

By United Press International

BOSTON, Nov. 16—Governor Furcolo said today although the appointment of President-elect

Above: The freighter *Exermont* headlined in the Cape Cod Standard-Times issue of November 16, 1960. The vessel was aground until pulled off the next day. **Below:** On December 10, 1960, the fishing vessel *Sharron & Louise* was near Nantucket in a heavy northeast storm. She was attempting to make the harbor when she was driven ashore on the north beach of the island. Her engine was salvaged and the hull was later hauled off by a crane. There were no injuries to any of her crew. *Photo from the collection of Paul C. Morris, Nantucket, Mass.*

Chapter Nine

When Mother Nature brews up a gale and a ship runs aground or someone off shore needs medical attention or a fishing boat springs a leak and needs pumps to keep afloat or, a thousand and one other things that can go wrong.....they call the Coast Guard. Today's Life Savers are armed with modern space age equipment. They can speed to the scene of a disaster and carry out rescues that would marvel their predecessors. The horses and beach carts have been replaced by four wheel drive trucks and helicopters. The coston signals and rockets have been updated by electronic apparatuses which enable today's Life Saver to communicate faster and more effectively than in the early days. If the *Josephus*, (Chapter One) which was wrecked in Truro in April, 1849, with the loss of twenty-five men, were to come ashore today, a Coast Guard helicopter from the Cape Cod Air station at Otis could lift the crew off and land them on shore without ever getting their feet wet. The United States Coast Guard is today a consolidation of four fundamental services under one command. The Aids to Navigation was formerly the Lighthouse Service. The Merchant Marine Safety Bureau was formerly the Bureau of Marine Inspection. The Law Enforcement section was originally the Revenue Cutter service formed in 1790. The Search and Rescue operations were formerly the Life Saving Service, often supported by the Revenue Cutter service. Ice Patrols in the north Atlantic and Oceanography were added to the myriad of duties in later developments of the service. When a Coast Guard cutter leaves port on patrol the unit may be required to carry out several of the above duties. The vessel may be requested to go to the aid of a ship in distress or to check an aid to navigation or arrest a ship carrying contraband. Their primary function, however, is search and rescue. A national search and rescue plan was drafted in 1956 to delineate areas of responsibility for coordination of efforts. In an emergency, the Coast Guard is able to call on all federal agencies for assistance. The Navy, Army, Civil Aeronautics Administration, Air Force, Civil Air Patrol, Federal Communications Commission and all state and local law enforcement agencies. This inter-agency use facilitates the use of the best communications and appropriate personnel to answer the distress call.

In the 19th century, the captain of a sailing vessel was lucky to have a few hours warning of an approaching storm. The falling barometer was sometimes his only indication of changing weather. Today's captain knows about storms days before they arrive and can prepare his vessel for heavy weather. Modern computer aided satellite reports give adequate warnings of oncoming killer storms. Current shipbuilding technology has resulted in improved operational capabilities in today's vessels. This aids in reducing accidents. The design, power and reliability of today's vessels provides the mariner with an automated ship to maintain his schedules at sea. There is a significant amount of ship traffic around Cape Cod today. Most of the larger vessels use the Cape Cod canal to travel between New York and Boston. Occasionally there are accidents reported in the waterway and on the approaches.

The numerous maritime accidents around Cape Cod invariably appear on the front pages of the local newspapers. On November 16, 1960, the American freighter *Exermont* ran aground in the Cape Cod Canal while on a passage during dense fog. The 452-foot vessel hit the bank opposite the Mass. Maritime Academy. When the tide dropped the ship canted over. Pictures and stories were featured in the local papers. The Coast Guard sent the cutter *Evergreen* to assist the vessel but she was hard on the bank. The next day, two Boston tug-boats pulled her free and she went on her way to New York City after marine inspectors cleared her. On December 26, 1961, the Coast Guard cutter *Acushnet* rescued ten men from the dredge CARTAGENA, 180 miles east of Cape Cod when a tow line parted. The dredge was being towed to Baltimore from Halifax, Nova Scotia, when she encountered heavy seas off the Cape. Her tug radioed for help and the *Acushnet* answered the call. Later when the weather improved, the Canadian tug-boat *Foundation Vigilant* was able to secure a line aboard the dredge and complete the voyage to Baltimore.

Above: The 5,290 ton Dutch freighter *Korendyk* lost her steering and rammed into the bulkhead at the east end of the Cape Cod Canal on April 21, 1962. The collision ripped out about twenty feet of sheathing and backfill but the ship suffered little damage other than some paint on the hull. **Below:** Damage to the bulkhead was substantial. The anchor of the 460 foot Rotterdam vessel was dropped to hold her in place until temporary repairs could be made to the steering. Traffic was held up for two hours while the vessel was repaired. The *Korendyk* then proceeded under her own power to Boston. *Photos by Gordon E. Caldwell, Hyannis, Mass.*

Above: The motor vessel *Martha's Vineyard* was on a passage through Woods Hole harbor on August 4, 1961, when she ran aground on the rocks. The ship lay there for 24 hours until she was hauled off by a New Bedford tug, assisted by a Coast Guard cutter. The former Steamship Authority vessel was stuck across the harbor from her previous home. *Photo courtesy of a friend.* **Below:** On March 1, 1964, the Liberian tanker *Amphialos* was battling a North Atlantic storm and heavy seas two hundred miles east of Cape Cod when the vessel broke in half. The bow section sank and the stern was taken in tow by the salvage tug *Curb* of the Merritt, Chapman and Scott Company of New York. The tow did not last long as the ship sank shortly afterward. The tow line can be seen hanging from the stern. Two men were lost and 34 rescued in the accident. *Photo courtesy of the U.S. Coast Guard, Boston, Mass.*

Above: The *S.S. Nobska* steaming into Woods Hole Harbor in the fog missed a buoy and went aground on Nonamesset Island just across the harbor from her dock on July 17, 1964. She lay grounded over one tide and was later pulled off by the Coast Buard. *Photo courtesy of a friend.* **Above:** The 455-foot freighter *South African Victory*, with a thirty degree list lay dead in the water battered by forty foot seas on January 24, 1966 about seventy-five miles northeast of Provincetown. The ship had a crew of 48 men and carried five passengers. The crew managed to regain power and was able to limp into Boston, escorted by three Coast Guard cutters. *Photo courtesy of the U.S. Coast Guard, Boston, Mass.*

Above: The flying lifeboats proved their worth many times at sea during emergencies. The amphibious helicopter HH-52A is shown hovering over the fishing vessel *Phantom* preparing to hoist an injured seaman aboard for a trip to the hospital on December 1, 1966. **Below:** A savage winter storm claimed two fishing vessels in the Atlantic on April 28th, 1967. Coast Guard planes, helicopters and cutters were carrying out search and rescue along the entire coastline. Three crewmen of the New Bedford fishing vessel *Noreen* hauled aboard a portable pump after it had been parachuted to them by a Coast Guard plane from the Salem air station. The *Noreen* had developed a leak and was in danger of sinking 73 miles SSE of Nantucket when the plane found them and dropped the pump. The vessel made it back to port safely but two others were lost with their entire crews. *Photos courtesy of the U.S. Coast Guard, Boston, Mass.*

Above: The ketch *Paula's Fancy* was wrecked near South Beach on Marthas Vineyard on November 4, 1966. The sixty-foot sailing vessel was bound to Bermuda from Marblehead when she ran into an Atlantic storm. The storm battered vessel ran aground early in the morning and the crew of five men and two women were able to wade ashore just before the vessel broke up on the beach. *Photo by Harvey S. Ewing, Edgartown, Massachusetts.* **Below:** Thirty-six crewmen aboard the Liberian oil tanker *Keo* were lost on November 5, 1969 when the vessel split in half during a northeast storm. Remnants of the vessel were found 120 miles southeast of Nantucket island. *Photo courtesy of the U.S. Coast Guard, Boston, Mass.*

Above: The Honorable Discharge from the United States Coast Guard was a handsome paper which most men framed and put up in their den. The art work signified the many duties performed by the men of the service. On the left, the lifeboat crew is pictured going to the rescue and on the right the Revenue Cutter was depicted steaming out to save the crews of ships in distress on either side of the eagle with the electronics of communication in his talons. **Below:** A full gale was blowing out of the southwest on November 30, 1963 and the Provincetown fishing vessel *Queen Mary* broke loose from her mooring and washed up on the beach. The next morning, waves broke over the stranded vessel. *Photo by Richard G. Christopher.*

The midget submarine ALVIN from the Woods Hole Oceanographic Institution was lost in 5,000 feet of water on October 16, 1968 when a cable broke during launching, 120 miles southeast of Cape Cod. This photograph was made of the sub on the bottom. ***Photo courtesy of the Woods Hole Oceanographic Institution***

On January 10, 1966 the New Bedford fishing vessel *Venture I* was fishing south of Martha's Vineyard when two of her crewmen were injured. The boat was taken in tow by a Russian fishing vessel and the two crewmen treated aboard the Soviet fish processing ship. The boat was then anchored, 30 miles south of Nantucket while the two men were taken off the Russian ship by a Coast Guard helicopter from Air Station Cape Cod. The *Venture I* was wrecked on Chatham Bars in August, 1982 and was a total loss.

A storm with winds of more than sixty miles an hour and seas topping twenty feet caused the loss of two New Bedford fishing boats off Cape Cod on April 29, 1967. A massive search was launched by the Coast Guard for the 94-foot trawler *Deep Waters* and the 191-foot *Elizabeth N.* A distress call from the second vessel said the trawler was being battered by 100 mile-an- hour winds and 35-foot waves. The vessels each had crews of six men from the New Bedford area and all were lost. On October 16, 1968 the Woods Hole Oceanographic Institution lost their deep diving miniature submarine ALVIN. The research vessel sank during a launching operation about 120 miles south of Cape Cod. A cable broke aboard the mother ship allowing the small sub to drop in the water. Her top hatch was open. She filled and sank in 4,500 feet of water near Hydrographers Canyon. A year later, on August 30, 1969 the deep diving research submarine ALUMINAUT found the ALVIN during a search and the small sub was recovered. The submarine was rebuilt and returned to service.

The sub was found by the research sub ALUMINAUT and hoisted to the surface by the research ship *Mizar.* It was brought to the deck for survey of damages. The undersea research vessel was repaired and continued research dives. Perhaps the most famous exploration by the small submarine ALVIN was in July 1986 when it went to survey the sunken liner *Titanic,* 13,000 feet down off the coast of Newfoundland. *Photo courtesy of the Woods Hole Oceanographic Institution.*

"Let's wait 'til the sharks are nipping his heels. If there's anything I hate, it's a dull and undramatic rescue."

The Coast Guard poked a little fun at the men who fly the rescue planes in the March 1957 issue of the U.S. Coast Guard Magazine. The magazine was published by the Army Times Publishing Company in Washington, D.C. It is obviously a caricature of the HU-16E Albatross amphibious aircraft.

The Coast Guard began to see the value of the airplane soon after it became practical. Some members of the Kill Devil Hills Lifeboat Station at Cape Hatteras assisted the Wright Brothers when they flew the first powered aircraft in December, 1903. It was obvious that an eye in the sky was invaluable for search and rescue operations out over the ocean. It was far superior to the lookouts atop the mast of a surface ship. Just before World War I the Coast Guard sent men to Pensacola, Florida to train in Navy planes. But it wasn't until 1925 that Congress appropriated money for Coast Guard air bases along the coast. The first two Coast Guard airfields were at Gloucester, Massachusetts and Cape May, New Jersey. The motive for the long awaited appropriations was the fight against the rum runners. The air arm gave the Coast Guard a lift-up in the battle against the smugglers.

The air operations of the Coast Guard have grown over the years until today, the service maintains one of the finest sea-rescue forces in the world. Yesterday's life-saver had to battle snow drifts on the beaches while hauling a heavy beach cart over the dunes to the scene of a shipwreck, rig the breeches buoy and bring men ashore wet and cold. Or they would launch a life-boat in heavy seas and row out to save survivors aboard foundering ships. Today the same tasks are performed by Coast Guard men in helicopters and jet aircraft, using space age technology, computer controlled navigation, sophisticated radar with tactical and infared detection devices. Today's life-saver can speed to the scene of a disaster, rescue the people and land them ashore in relative safety.

Above: The Albatross, HU-16E amphibious aircraft served long in the air arm of the U.S. Coast Guard. This plane was phased out and retired from the service in March, 1983. *Photo by the Author.* **Below:** The new Guardian, HU-25A jet is a modern sophisticated aircraft to replace the Albatross and will fly the search and rescue missions from the Cape Cod Air Station. *Photo by Gordon Caldwell, Hyannis, Massachusetts.*

Above: The fishing vessel *Northern Lights* went aground in Buzzards Bay about 300 yards from the entrance to the Cape Cod Canal on September 15, 1970. The boat was out of Point Judith, Rhode Island with a crew of six men. She had a load of ice in her hold and when the melting ice was removed the vessel floated free. *Photo courtesy of a friend.*
Below: On December 18, 1973, the Greek tanker *Armonia* grounded on the rip-rap in the Cape Cod Canal at Bournedale. Tricky currents were the cause of the accident and the ship suffered a gash in her bow below the water line. The vessel was in no danger and was able to continue her trip when pulled off the rocks by the tugs. *Photo by the Author.*

Chapter Ten

In 1903, Marconi worked with a crude "spark-gap" transformer and gave birth to the communications industry. The radio has developed from a fledgling business to a giant industry. The popularity of television has stimulated a phenomenal expansion in electronics, presenting live pictures of entertainment, news and sports in the living rooms of this country's homes. It has precipitated a significant social change in our nation. The electronic industry is comprised of the radio and television broadcast systems with international signals transmitted over satellite networks. Also world wide communications, missile guidance systems and computers. Satellites placed in orbit around the earth aid mariners aboard ship to pin-point their location in mid-ocean. Recent technology has improved safety at sea but electronics play a major role in martime operations today. The gyrocompass took much of the guesswork out of navigation and enabled ships to steer a more true course. Sonar was used in World War I to detect submarines but was erratic, and not dependable, until scientists discovered the thermoclines. In World War II the sonar was helpful in detecting enemy submarines. Further advances in sonar enable fishing vessels to find schools of fish underwater.

A valuable tool for operational safety was perfected in World War II. Radar was primarily designed to detect enemy aircraft during wartime. It is a beam of electronic impulses which bounce off metal targets and these appear as blips on a receiver screen. There are many types of radar in use today. Most ships are equipped with a navigational type. Weather radar also plots storms for improved forecasting. There are various other types of electronics which aid the mariner at sea today. Loran, or long range navigation, is a radio direction system which determines a ship's location at sea. By using loran charts, the data is automatically computed to establish a ship's position. The space age has brought fourth satellite navigation. The satellites orbit 600 miles above the earth and continuously broadcast their positions. The computers aboard ship are able to determine the latitude and longitude of the vessel from the satellite signals. This system has now relegated the traditional instruments of celestial navigation to the dark ages. A navigator today, is no longer really needed aboard ship except as a backup to the electronic systems.

In 1973, the Coast Guard discontinued coverage of three off-shore weather stations in the Atlantic. Ocean stations Bravo, Charlie and Delta had been patrolled for more than 25 years but meteorological, navigation and communications satellites had rendered them obsolete. The stations were covered by 255-foot cutters. The patrols were isolated and lonely, but the tour usually lasted for only one month. If it was during one of the winter months, the patrol was cold and stormy. The closing of the off-shore stations helped to reduce the onus on the Coast Guard and relieved the ships and men for other duties.

On June 27, 1973, the fishing vessel *Miss Casey* was at work in heavy seas eighty miles south of Martha's Vineyard when a couple of large waves swamped the boat. The Captain, Richard B. Allen sent out SOS signals over the radio. The vessel sank until her decks were awash. Capt. Allen and his crewman Peter Stoeckle climbed atop the wooden roof of the cabin as the rough weather continued. Air spaces inside the hull apparently prevented the boat from going to the bottom and the two men spent the night trying to attract the attention of passing vessels with their searchlight. Several ships went by, but none of them stopped to help the stranded men. The two spent 24 hours perched atop the sunken hull. The first sign of help was a Russian factory ship. The *Nikolai Danilov* came along and rescued the two Americans. The Soviet ship then rigged a sling under the *Miss Casey* and lifted the boat out of the water. The Coast Guard cutter *Tamora* arrived on scene and pumped the water out of the small vessel. Later the cutter towed the fishing vessel along with her grateful crew back to Point Judith.

In early February, 1974, an oil barge grounded near Sandy Neck beach in Barnstable after strong northeast winds caused the towing hawser to break. In this series of six photographs, the barge is shown on the beach with a large crowd of people gathered to watch the operations. A Coast Guard helicopter flew up over the Bouchard Barge Number 105 and picked up the hawser.

The chopper then carried the hawser out to a 44-foot motor lifeboat a short way off shore. The lifeboat then pulled the hawser out to the tugboat and at high tide the tug eased the barge off the beach. In the final photograph the Moran tug and barge are shown passing through the Cape Cod Canal headed for New York. *Photographs by Gordon E. Caldwell, Hyannis, Mass.*

Above: At the northern tip of Monomoy Island, the remains of a small vessel washed out of the sands in 1970. The bones were either from a fishing boat or small sailing vessel. The age could not be determined. In the photo (back to,) Cape Cod National Seashore Historian Mike Whatley made some photos for the files as Don St. Pierre of Chatham inspected the remains. Thousands of hulks similar to this are buried all along the backside of Cape Cod.**Below:** The Soviet research vessel *Belogorsk* ran up on a stone jetty in Woods Hole harbor on September 3, 1974. The ship was in the U.S. to take part in a cooperative fisheries research program. She was assisted off the rocks without damage by the Coast Guard tug *Towline* and she tied up at the Woods Hole Oceanographic Institute pier. *Photos by the Author.*

Above: The ten meter sloop *Trull* ran aground on Sandy Neck in Barnstable on the night of October 27, 1974, while fighting heavy seas in Cape Cod Bay. The Coast Guard rescued the crew by helicopter. The boat lay helpless on her side at low water. It would appear in the photograph that the modern day Cape Cod mooncussers were gathered around her on the beach. *Photo by P.T. Wolf, courtesy of the Yarmouth Register.* **Below:** A couple days later the vessel lay stripped and gutted. The local mooncussers had done their damage well and all the owner had left was a smashed hull and broken dreams. *Photo by Gordon E. Caldwell, Hyannis, Mass.*

Above: The New Bedford fishing vessel *Algarve II* lost her bearings in a storm on the night of November 25, 1974, and ran up on the rock jetty at the entrance to Nantucket harbor. The three man crew was rescued by a Coast Guard Helicopter and the vessel was a total loss. This photo was made much later as the hull was used for a local film production about Coast Guard operations around Cape Cod. *Photo by Chief Charles Moore, U.S.C.G.* **Below:** The hull of the *Algarve II* was later picked up by a salvage barge and taken to New Bedford where it was stripped of all usable parts. *Photo by S. J. Turner, North Dartmouth, Mass.*

Above: This is the bow section of a wrecked fishing boat on Nauset Beach in Orleans. The wreckage is unidentified. There were several wrecks during this period and it could have been any one of many. **Below:** The stern section of the fishing vessel with the rudder sticking up in the air. When fishing vessels are wrecked on the back side, they usually break up and the pieces are moved by the currents. They end up, sanded in along the shore and sometimes are discovered years later. *Photos courtesy of K.W. Winslow, Chestnut Hill, Mass.*

Above & Below: The Liberian tanker *Spartan Lady* broke in half in heavy seas 150 miles south of Cape Cod on April 4, 1975. The bow section floated away from the stern and was sunk by the Coast Guard. The cargo of one half million gallons of oil was lost. *Photos courtesy of the U. S. Coast Guard.*

Above: The crew of the tanker *Spartan Lady* gathered on the stern when the Coast Guard helicopters arrived to pick them up. The helicopters lowered baskets from 100 feet off the deck during winds clocked at 50 knots.*Photo courtesy of the U.S. Coast Guard.* **Below:** Survivors of the tanker wreck were landed at Barnstable Airport on Cape Cod. One man was lost to a heart failure during the flight in from the scene. One man fell to his knees to thank the Almighty for his rescue. The others were just happy to reach dry land. *Photo by Lou La Prade.*

Above: On June 7, 1975, the New Bedford fishing vessel *Theresa and Jean* was being towed into port by the Coast Guard cutter *Tamora*, after she had broken her propeller shaft and began to leak. The water rose too fast for the pumps and the vessel started to sink. A Coast Guard helicopter took the crew of six off the boat and men from the cutter tried to keep the fishing vessel afloat but, because of high seas and foul weather, had to abandon her. The *Theresa and Jean* sank fifteen miles east of Cape Cod. *Photo courtesy of the U.S. Coast Guard.* **Below:** The cement barge *Angela* was wrecked on the Hens and Chickens, south of Westport, Mass, in Buzzards Bay on March 4, 1971. The barge was at anchor when a squall caused her to swing around and drag onto the ledge. Leaks solidified the cement cargo and the vessel became a total loss. Five years later on May 5, 1976, the barge *Centennial II* went aground at the same spot during a storm. The container barge had a three million dollar cargo aboard. Her crew was removed and the next day a crew of salvors from Falmouth boarded the barge by helicopter and began salvage. The case ended up in court and on May 20th the barge broke up and sank in high winds before all of her cargo had been removed. *Aerial photo by the Author.*

The New Bedford fishing vessel *Sylvester F. Whalen* came ashore on Cisco Beach on Nantucket Island on November 4, 1976. The 91-foot fisherman was returning from Georges Bank and had developed a bad leak. Electrical power was lost and when pumps could not keep her afloat, the Captain decided to beach his vessel. The Coast Guard removed the crew of six by helicopter and the fishing boat was a total loss. *Photo by Jeff Barnard, Nantucket, Mass.*

On December 15, 1976, the Liberian tanker *Argo Merchant* grounded on the shoals, twenty-nine miles southeast of Nantucket Island. On the 16th, the Coast Guard cutter *Vigilant* arrived on the scene to control salvage operations. *Photo by the Author.*

The concerns by environmentalists about oil spills by ocean going tankers were intensified in 1967 when the supertanker *Torrey Canyon* grounded and broke in two off Lands End, the southwestern point of the British Islands. Millions of gallons of crude oil washed up on the beaches of Cornwall. The ecological damage was in the millions of dollars and headlines all over the world publicized the event. The accident was a harbinger of many more to come on both sides of the Atlantic. In December, 1976, the Liberian tanker *Argo Merchant* ran up on the Nantucket Shoals, 29 miles southeast of the island and six days later broke in two, spilling seven and a half million gallons of bunker oil into the Atlantic Ocean.

A little over a month after the *Argo Merchant* grounding the Bouchard oil barge Number 65 ran aground in Buzzards Bay off Wings Neck and spilled one hundred thousand gallons of fuel oil. Attempts were made to clean up the spill but the huge ice field that caused the grounding also hampered their efforts. The Coast Guard tried to burn some of the oil with a wicking agent atop the ice but the experiment failed. Another tanker, this one with almost ten million gallons of gasoline, ran up on Davis Bank off Nantucket on January 20, 1979. The British tanker *Afghanistan* ran aground about ten miles northwest of where the *Argo Merchant* grounded in 1976. Cause of the accident was blamed on a "wrong turn" acording to Coast Guard officials investigating the incident. Coast Guard Captain Barry Eldridge said: "It appears they made a mistake in identifying a buoy and made the wrong turn on it." The vessel was grounded for about an hour when the tide lifted her and she backed off the shoal area. A Coast Guard 41 foot boat led the ship back to deeper water through the dangerous shoals. The ship was enroute from the Virgin Islands to Boston with a crew of 41 persons.

Above: A Coast Guard helicopter hovered over the grounded tanker while ferrying salvage personnel to and from the ship. *Photo courtesy of the U.S. Coast Guard.* **Below:** Six days after running aground the *Argo Merchant* broke in half in bad weather and spilled over seven million gallons of heavy black oil into the Atlantic. *Photo by Gordon E. Caldwell, Hyannis, Mass.*

Above: The oil barge Bouchard B No. 65, carrying 3.3 million gallons of home heating oil, ran aground off Wings Neck in Buzzards Bay on the night of January 28, 1977. The cargo tanks were ruptured and leaking. Another barge was brought alongside to unload the cargo. **Below:** The oil from the barge Bouchard B No. 65, drifted around in Buzzards Bay. To avoid further pollution, the Coast Guard attempted to burn the oil with a wicking agent atop the ice. Some oil was burned but the smoke was worse than the oil. *Photos by the Author.*

Above: The British trawler *Croesus* ran aground off Tuckernuck Island, near Nantucket on January 16, 1977. The boat came over from Hull, England and was being delivered to Nova Scotia when she got lost in a blinding snowstorm. The Coast Guard removed the crew of three by a lifeboat from the Brant Point station on Nantucket. The trawler lay on the shoal all winter and was badly damaged by ice floes. The 78-foot hull was a total loss. *Aerial Photograph by the Author.* **Below:** Crewmen on board the Cypriot freighter *Agios Nicolaus K* are shown on deck working to secure five one-ton cylinders of liquid chlorine. The ship was underway from St. Johns, N.B. to Cuba, when the deadly cargo broke loose in heavy seas. The U.S. Coast Guard granted permission for the ship to enter Cape Cod Bay to tie down the loose cargo. The ship anchored in the middle of the bay on March 27, 1978, and the work was completed in calm waters. The ship departed without incident on March 29th. *Aerial photo by the late Richard C. Kelsey, Chatham, Mass.*

Above: On February 18, 1979, four airmen aboard a Coast Guard helicopter were killed when their aircraft crashed into the Atlantic Ocean. The chopper was on a rescue mission 180 miles southeast of Cape Cod in thick weather. The sea was rough and, at the time of the accident, the aircraft was hovering over a fishing vessel to remove an injured crewman. A huge wave struck the nose of the aircraft on the right side and it rolled into the sea. One airman from the helicopter survived. *Photo courtesy of the U.S. Coast Guard.* **Below:** On June 18, 1979, the tanker *Exxon Chester* rammed the Liberian freighter *Regal Sword* in dense fog about 30 miles southeast of Chatham lighthouse. The freighter sank in the Atlantic and her crew of 38 men cleared in a lifeboat just as she went down. They were all picked up by the tanker and taken to Boston. On arrival in the Hub, crew members of the *Regal Sword* said that the two lookouts on the bridge were both below having supper at the time of the accident. The photo shows the tanker with a smashed bow. *Photo courtesy of a friend.*

Above: A close call for a Greek cargo ship in the waters south of Nantucket on February 2, 1979. The ship radioed the Coast Guard that she was taking on water. The water had flooded one of three cargo holds aboard the vessel about 70 miles southeast of the island. The American tanker *Fort Worth* stood by, ready to help but a Coast Guard cutter and helicopter guided the *Lygaria* into Providence, Rhode Island after the Master had regained control of the flooding. *Photo by Lt.jg J. Currier, U.S. Coast Guard.* **Below:** One of the scenes of the times was television film cameramen at work during disasters and news events. In the photo, Jerry Small on the left and the Author (right) wind their cameras while shooting a story from inside a Coast Guard Helicopter. Another photographer captured the scene during coverage of a routine story out over the ocean near Nantucket Island. *Photo courtesy of the U.S. Coast Guard, Boston, Mass.*

Above: The Gold Medal lifeboat CG36500 is a floating museum around southern New England waters in the summertime. The Boat is presently preserved in the water and is shown at maritime displays throughout the southern New England area. *Photo by the Author.* **Below:** On May 10, 1986 the famous rescue boat CG-36500 sank at her mooring in Chatham harbor. The accident was a combination of high winds and an opposing strong tide. There was no one aboard at the time and it was believed that a faulty automatic bilge pump failed and allowed the boat to fill with water. The recently restored boat was used in the historic rescue of 32 men off the tanker *Pendleton* in February 1952. Salvagers raised the vessel and it was again restored to working condition. *Photo by Ben Barnhart, courtesy of the Cape Codder, Orleans, Mass.*

Chapter Eleven

On the night of February 18, 1952, two tankers broke in half off the backside of Cape Cod. A thirty-six foot motor lifeboat from the Chatham Coast Guard Station, went out in blizzard conditions and saved 32 men off the stern section of the tanker *Pendleton* in a spectacular rescue. The boat was retired from the service in 1968 and turned over to the Cape Cod National Seashore for preservation. It was to be included in a proposed museum for Coast Guard memorabilia. The museum was too small for the large vessel and it fell into disrepair while stored outside the maintenance garages in Wellfleet.

In an effort to preserve a notable piece of Cape Cod maritime history, negotiations for the transfer of ownership of the boat were completed in late October, 1981 and the boat became the property of the Orleans Historical Society. The craft was brought to Orleans for restoration. This work was accomplished by volunteers in the winter of 1981-1982. The boat was launched at Rock Harbor in May of 1982. The CG36500 remains in the water year round, a floating museum dedicated to the Lifesavers of Cape Cod. Winter storage is at the Stage Harbor Marina in Chatham. The Orleans Historical Society is guardian of the craft but she belongs to the people of Cape Cod. The small vessel makes a tour of southeastern New England ports each summer manned by the Coast Guard Auxiliary. She is maintained by volunteers; members of the Society and other interested persons. The boat is hauled out of the water each spring for painting and other repairs necessary to keep her operational. The costs of running the boat and her maintenance are borne by funds donated by summer visitors viewing the boat on tour and by other annual gifts.

Todays beachcomber is no longer dependent on the flotsam and jetsam for his livelihood. He walks the outer beach to find treasures such as a colorful lobster pot buoy or perhaps if he is lucky, a lobster pot might come ashore in a storm and be tossed high and dry where the beach picker might throw it in the back of his dune buggy and carry it home for a backyard decoration. Yesterday's beachcomber would find a new set of rules along this strand since the creation of the Cape Cod National Seashore. The beaches today are used chiefly for bathing and sunning, not beachcombing. Metal detectors are not allowed on any Federally controlled beach area. The flotsam and jetsam can be picked up but old wood is forbidden. This is a result of the antiquities act of 1916 which prohibits the removal of any pieces of a ship which are fifty years old or older. The restricted areas are primarily within the boundaries of the National Seashore.

Above: The ferry *Islander* at the pier in Oak Bluffs on Martha's Vineyard Island after it hit a submerged object on March 19, 1980 and damaged her hull in five places. The veteran ferry had just left the dock when the accident occurred. Captain Antone Jardin immediately return the vessel to the slip without injury to any of the passengers. **Below:** An aerial view of the ferry *Islander* at the slip at Oak Bluffs. Fire trucks from six island towns rushed to the pier to assist in pumping out the ship while the automobiles were taken off.

The ferry *Islander* at her slip in Oak Bluffs after the accident. Emergency crews carried six inch suction hoses to pump out the bilges and keep the vessel afloat while the cargo of automobiles was off-loaded. The ferry was out of service for a few weeks while repairs were made to her hull.

Above: On February 26, 1981, the Norwegian freighter *Norcan* lost power while passing through the Cape Cod Canal. The vessel was on her way to New Bedford with a cargo of frozen fish. The crew dropped anchor while repairs were made and the Army Corps patrol boat assisted a tugboat while the ship was at anchor. Repairs were made and the vessel resumed her voyage. *Photo by Cindy Towne, Cape Cod Independent, Buzzards Bay, Mass.* **Below:** The motor vessel *Auriga* was underway in dense fog on August 10, 1981 about two miles outside Woods Hole harbor when she was in collision with the steamer *Naushon*. The bow of the freight vessel was stove in and was extensively damaged. *Photo by the Author.*

Above: The fishing vessel *Virginia Kadet* ran up on some rocks and then sank off Cuttyhunk Island on August 18, 1981. The steel hulled vessel was on passage from Newport, Rhode Island, to Georges Bank when the mishap occurred. The fifteen man crew spent five hours during the night in life rafts before being picked up by a passing yacht. The Coast Guard rigged a floating oil containment boom around the craft to enable clean up crews to pump off the twelve thousand gallons of fuel. The vessel was later refloated and towed into a Fairhaven shipyard. *Aerial photo by the Author.*
Below: The New Bedford fishing vessel *Little Growler* sprung a leak in Nantucket Sound on April 29, 1982. The boat tied up to a buoy on Cross Rip shoal and the Coast Guard helicopter dropped a pump to assist the men aboard the vessel. A 41-foot motor boat from the Brant Point station stood by while the crew pumped out the flooded bilges. The *Little Growler* later limped back to port safely. *Aerial Photo by Gordon E. Caldwell, Hyannis, Mass.*

Above: Chatham Bars claimed another victim early in the morning on August 9, 1982 when the 73-foot New Bedford fishing vessel *Venture I* ran aground about a mile south of the Chatham inlet. The Coast Guard battled six to eight foot seas to remove the five man crew. *Photo by the late Richard C. Kelsey, Chatham, Mass.* **Below:** Salvagers from the lower Cape area soon picked the vessel clean and less than a month the pounding waves had reduced the hull to less than firewood. *Aerial Photo by the Author.*

Above: On October 11, 1982, Coast Guardsmen from the cutter *Vigorous* passed a line to sailors aboard the trimaran *Gonzo* that had capsized 300 miles east of Cape Cod in the Atlantic. A distress signal from the boat's emergency locator transmitter was picked up by a Soviet search-and-rescue satellite orbiting above the earth at 600 miles per hour. In 1970, Congress passed a law requiring general aviation aircraft to carry an emergency locator transmitter that would automatically emit a signal under the typical stress of an accident. Since then the National Transportation Safety Board has recommended that all ocean going craft carry this equipment. The results are shown in the photograph above. **Below:** A routine rescue at sea on March 30, 1983 occurred when a crewman fell through a hatch aboard the fishing vessel *Eileen D.*, out of New Bedford. A Coast Guard helicopter from Cape Cod Air Base lifted the man aboard while the vessel was thirty miles southeast of Nantucket and brought him to Cape Cod hospital in Hyannis where he was treated for a fractured ankle and then released. *Photos courtesy of the U.S. Coast Guard.*

Above: The Woods Hole based Coast Guard cutter *Cape Henlopen* escorted the fishing trawler *C. & S. Smile* into Boston harbor after the vessel was seized 40 miles northeast of Provincetown on April 6, 1983. The cutter proudly displayed the flag with a marijuana leaf depicted on it, a symbol of an arrest. **Below:** This arrest was unique in that a woman was in command of the Coast Guard cutter at the time of the apprehension. Lt. j.g. Susan K. Donner became the first woman to command a cutter in the First Coast Guard District in June of 1982. Lt. Donner is shown on deck with one of her eleven male crewmen. *Photos by S.N. Norm Whitehurst, U.S. Coast Guard.*

Above: The *Morton S. Bouchard, Jr.* sank in the west end of the Cape Cod Canal near the Bourne Bridge on April 11, 1983. The 100-foot tugboat capsized when it became tangled in the tow cable running to a barge it was towing. The accident happened at night and the seven man crew were all rescued by the two men on the barge. A heavy oil slick spread out throughout the canal and efforts were made to control the spill. **Below:** The barge Century lifted the sunken tug off the bottom of the canal a week later and it was towed to a shipyard for repairs. *Photos by the Author.*

Above: The 123-foot Spanish fishing dragger *Tasarte* ran aground in the Tuckernuck Bank area between Nantucket and Martha's Vineyard shortly before midnight on August 11, 1983. Crew members lashed two life-rafts together and abandoned ship. They were later picked up by the Coast Guard. The Captain radioed his position and later the grounded vessel was pulled off with little damage. *Photo by Ens. F.W. Tucher, USCGC Bittersweet.* **Below:** The *Falcon*, out of New Bedford was passing through the Cape Cod Canal on April 1st, 1984 when the steering gear malfunctioned. The boat drifted on the rocks and listed over to port when the tide dropped. The crew was removed by the Corps of Engineers patrol vessel and the fishing boat refloated at high tide and was towed back to New Bedford. *Photo by Gordon E. Caldwell, Hyannis, Mass.*

Above: On March 29, 1985, the Maltese freighter *Eldia* was on a passage from St. John, New Brunswick to Norfolk, Virginia. When she passed the tip of Cape Cod she ran into a fierce northeast storm with gale force winds and high seas. The vessel had little ballast and was at the mercy of the high winds. With both anchors dragging the ship came ashore on Nauset Beach in Orleans. *Photo by Greg O'Brien, Courtesy of the Cape Codder, Orleans, Mass.* **Below:** Late in the afternoon with waves breaking over her stern the Captain radioed to the Coast Guard for assistance. The call was answered by men from the Chatham Coast Guard station and a helicopter from Air Station Cape Cod. As the bow of the ship slid up on shore, a large crowd gathered on the beach to watch the rescue take place. *Photo by the Author.*

Above: The helicopter from Air Station Cape Cod rescued 23 crewmen from the stranded freighter *Eldia* late in the afternoon in 80 knot winds. The crewmen were picked up in the basket and landed on the beach. *Photo by the Author.* **Below:** The helicopter landed at Nauset Beach parking lot where the crew of the *Eldia* were transferred to waiting ambulances. *Photo by Greg O'Brien, courtesy of the Cape Codder, Orleans, Mass.*

A few days after the grounding, weekend traffic to and from the beach in Orleans was jammed to capacity. This aerial view shows the parking lot almost full and the line of cars trying to get in, stretching back beyond the top of the hill. *Photo by the Author.*

The economic impact of a shipwreck on the outer shores of Cape Cod has only changed in substance. In the 19th century, a grounded vessel was sometimes refloated by Cape Cod wreckers and they were paid well for their labors. A shipwreck at that time, was salvage and many local men became rich recovering cargoes and stripping wrecks. Today a wreck on the beach brings an avalanche of sightseers. As a result, the local cash registers ring loud with tourist dollars. An example can be taken from the grounding of the Maltese freighter *Eldia* on March 29, 1984 on Nauset Beach in Orleans during a northeast storm. Photographs of the ship trapped on the Cape sands were front page news. It was featured on television newscasts all over New England. The curious flocked to the shoreline for a first hand look at the grounded freighter. The vessel lay on the sand about a mile from the parking lot at Nauset Beach and was readily accessible to the large crowds that walked down the shore to see it.

The sightseeing crowd continued almost every day until the vessel was pulled off the beach. Picture souvenirs in the form of T-shirts, coffee mugs and post cards appeared almost instantly on the store shelves. They were snatched up as collectibles by everyone who journeyed down to view the grounded vessel. The *Eldia* was pulled off the beach by salvagers on May 17, 1984 after being aground for 49 days. The ship was towed around the back side of Cape Cod into the Bay. The next day she was towed through the canal and then on to Newport, Rhode Island to a shipyard for dry-docking and determination of repairs. The ship laid alongside the pier for four years. In April of 1989 she was towed to New Jersey to be cut up for scrap.

Above: The *Eldia* lay on the sands like a beached whale. Salvage efforts were begun and lasted for weeks. In the meantime, the crowds continued to walk down to look at the vessel. Local entrepreneurs made a killing selling souvenirs to the tourists; post cards, t-shirts and coffee mugs were among the many different items on the market. *Aerial Photo by the Author.* **Below:** The cars filled the parking lot each day and the tourists walked about a mile to get a close up look at the grounded *Eldia*. Concern for the dunes caused officials to close the trails and direct the foot traffic down the outside beach. *Photo by Ben Barnhart, courtesy of the Cape Codder, Orleans, Mass.*

Above: Television news was present throughout the entire episode. This photo was made on May 16th after the ship had been turned around prior to refloating. The weird looking apparatus on top of the station wagon in the foreground is a television microwave sending unit. Two Boston stations covered the grounding from start to finish. The *Eldia* was pulled off at 3 a.m. on May 17, 1984 and towed to Newport Rhode Island for repairs at a local shipyard. *Photo by the Author.* **Below:** The *Eldia* lay at the Rhode Island shipyard until the summer of 1989 when she was towed by a Moran tug to a New Jersey shipbreakers yard to be cut up for scrap metal. *Photo by Francis J. Duffy, courtesy of the Moran Towing Company.*

Above: On June 13, 1984 the fishing vessel *Lady of Grace* caught fire while fishing 75 miles southeast of Cape Cod. Her six man crew abandoned ship in lifeboats and were later picked up. The Coast Guard cutter *Bibb* was 17 miles away and she answered the call for help. **Below:** Men from the cutter sprayed water on the burning hull and cooled it down enough to place canisters of foam on board. After the fire was extinguished the boat was taken in tow by the cutter *Cape Henlopen* and brought to port. *Photos courtesy of the U.S. Coast Guard.*

The 52-foot schooner *Reveler* lay sunk in front of the 230-foot steel hull ferry *Nantucket* on July 9, 1984 after a collision in the entrance channel to Hyannis harbor. The boat had been on a parallel course to the ferry when suddenly it veered right in front of the large vessel. The accident sent the small schooner to the bottom and her crew swam to shore. There were no injuries and a few days later the boat was raised. *Photo by Gordon E. Caldwell, Hyannis, Mass.*

Scattered along the bottom of Cape Cod Bay, Buzzards Bay, around Nantucket or Vineyard sounds and along the Atlantic shoreline lie the remains of thousands of shipwrecks. There are vast amounts of wreckage and old hulls that are explored by divers looking for various treasures. Their expeditions begin with research. The information lies buried in the archives of museums, old newspapers and eye-witness accounts about the 18th and 19th century wrecks. Before the days of radar and computer navigation, ship captains used to hug the coastline while bound between the ports of New York and Boston. In storms and fogs, many of these coastal ships met their fate along the shoals and in the bays around Cape Cod. The several sailing vessels outlined in earlier chapters are but a fraction of the total around this area. Today, amateur divers practice their hobby on weekends in these waters. Scientists and archaeologists are among the growing number of professional people engaged in SCUBA diving. Some of the valuable finds on the bottom are brass portholes, steering wheels, binnacles, bells and propellers. The amateur diver usually explores known wreck areas while the more experienced hunters look for sunken hulls that have never before been discovered.

Todays salvagers no longer rely on chance to find shipwrecks. The use of new scientific instruments is widespread, not only for searching the sea floor but beneath the shifting sands on the bottom. Side scan sonar emits an acoustic beam which is narrow in the horizontal and wide in the vertical planes. This beam is projected out across the sea floor and by receiving reflected echoes, prints a remarkably accurate picture of the sea bed and the objects lying on it. In order to probe down under the ocean floor, the magnetometer is used. It can sense anomalies in the earth's magnetic field as it is affected by ferrous objects that are buried under the surface. The use of side scan sonar by divers in search of sunken wrecks on the bottom has turned up discoveries from Cape Cod to Florida. Some of the treasure salvagers have been eminently successful while others are still looking.

Above: The fishing vessel *Maureen S.* ran aground about 3 a.m. on the morning of January 20, 1985, near Gay Head beach on Martha's Vineyard Island. The Coast Guard removed the five man crew by helicopter and landed them at Falmouth. The vessel was pulled off three days later by a tug. **Below:** The barge Richard K., with 840,000 gallons of gasoline, was adrift off the Rhode Island coast on January 20, 1985 after a cable broke from her tug. A Coast Guard helicopter from Air Station Cape Cod hovered over the barge, four and a half miles northwest of Block Island until it was reattached by towline to her tug and towed to Providence, R.I. *Photos courtesy of the U.S. Coast Guard, Boston, Mass.*

Chapter Twelve

There are perhaps several reasons for saving unique items of maritime antiquity. It is believed that man evolved from the sea in the primeval millenniums. His blood has a similar chemical composition to that of sea water. In addition, while growing up, young men are exposed to sea stories when they read various classics like Treasure Island and Moby Dick. Whatever the reason, man has never been separated from his roots in old ocean.

Maritime antiques hold a unique spell over the collector in his quest for the oldest artifacts. The list of collectables is wide and varied. The most popular item is the ship model. It is the oldest form of marine memorabilia and a beautiful model is the pride of any collection. Other general artifacts include sea chests, paintings, rigging hardware, navigation equipment and scrimshaw. Collectors find their treasures at auctions primarily but some find items at flea markets and estate sales. There are collectors who specialize in certain fields. Some buy only sailing ship items while others collect only articles from steamboats. There are several purists who want only artifacts from shipwrecks. These materials are usually purchased from divers who search along the bottom off-shore for bronze or other artifacts not eroded by sea water.

One of the more popular items is the marine painting. The artists of yesterday created masterpieces on canvas of the magnificent clipper ships or other vessels under full sail with fair winds and a bone in their teeth. These works of art always bring a high figure when they come on the auction block. Another artistic form is the figurehead. Carvings of men and women that once decorated the bows of sailing ships. Old navigation instruments are valuable items among the collectables. There are several in this category. Chronometers are perhaps the most expensive but octants, sextants, quadrants and barometers as well as binnacles and the ancient astrolabes bring respectable prices at maritime sales.

There are more items in the long list of marine antiques. Among these are whistles, running lights, lanterns, candleholders, rum kegs, liquor cabinets, strong boxes, bells, horns, anchors, portholes, telescopes, cannons, and ship's wheels. Articles in the paper field include old charts, logbooks, journals, seamen's diaries, maps and old ship registers. Nineteenth century newspaper reports on ship movements and shipwrecks are interesting and valuable. Whaling items are in a class by themselves. Harpoons, lances, cutting out tools all bring high prices but the most money is realized in the sale of scrimshaw, the ancient sailors artform carved out of the jawbone or teeth of a whale. Some of the items acquired are used to decorate homes or businesses. Weekend sailors have been known to decorate their offices so they may enjoy their hobby while at work. There are some dealers that specialize in only marine antiques. Several books have been written on the art of collecting in the maritime field. It might be interesting to look into the future and see what values are placed on old Loran sets when they come on the auction block. Undoubtedly, someone will find a way to display these along with much of the rest of the contemporary marine artifacts.

Above: The crew of the sixty-foot fishing boat *Kathryn Marie* radioed to the Coast Guard that they were sinking in Cape Cod Bay, five miles northeast of the canal in July, 1985. The Coast Guard crew at the canal station were standing by their boat for an inspection when the call came. **Below:** Within minutes two 41-foot patrol boats were on scene but the crew had abandoned the vessel into an aluminum boat. A Coast Guard helicopter captured these two photographs as the boat sank to the bottom. *Photos courtesy of the U.S. Coast Guard, Boston, Mass.*

Above: A sunken ghost ship was discovered in Cape Cod Bay off the coast of Wellfleet on August 21, 1985. The vessel was loaded with marijuana and had been scuttled. Coast Guard divers recovered the pot and seven men believed to be connected with the ship were arrested in a stake-out in Provincetown two days later. *Photo by Gordon E. Caldwell, Hyannis, Mass.* **Below:** A salvage crew raised the sunken ghost vessel later and the boat had the name of a legitimate Provincetown fishing vessel on her side: DIVINO CRIADOR. The vessel was sold at public auction to help pay the expenses in prosecuting the crime. *Photo courtesy of the U.S. Coast Guard, Boston, Massachusetts.*

The 70-foot fishing vessel *Champion Sea*, out of Point Judith, R.I. began taking on water about 15 miles west of Gay Head, Martha's Vineyard on December 13, 1985. A helicopter from Air Station Cape Cod dropped pumps to the boat and two 41-foot utility boats from the Coast Guard stations at Menemsha and Point Judith answered the call. They assisted the crew of the fishing vessel in saving their boat. The *Champion Sea* was towed to its home port for repairs. *Photo courtesy of the U.S. Coast Guard.*

Recently, off the coast of Wellfleet, salvagers claim to have found the remains of the pirate ship *Whidah.* As was expected, the possibility of finding a pirate treasure brought expanded and sometimes extravagant media coverage. The story began in December 1982, when the salvors staged an elaborate event. They sent divers to a spot off shore in Wellfleet and legally arrested the wreck. Over the months that followed the value of the treasure grew from two hundred to over four hundred million dollars.

The *Whidah* was wrecked in a storm on April 26, 1717. The remains have laid on the bottom since that time. The entire crew, save two, perished in the wreck. There have been many legends as to the booty and what happened to it. The records show that there were several wreckers at the beach on the morning following the storm. This fact may have a bearing on the amount of treasure yet to be recovered. The two surviving members of the crew testified that a treasure was on board when the ship was wrecked. No evidence has been forthcoming to disprove their story. The early Cape Codders may or may not have recovered some or all of the treasure.

The salvors, working with an old map, located a large amount of artifacts in the area being worked. A salvage vessel with large propeller deflectors began blasting holes in the bottom, moving sand away from the wreckage. Five years of work produced thousands of silver coins, several ancient artifacts such as tableware, hand guns and cannons. It was reported that they had found 47 cannon around the wreck site. The *Whidah* was a three hundred ton galley. This type of vessel could support 18 or 21 small cannon at the most. Forty-seven would have been a profusion of gunnery on a ship of that size. In October, 1985, a bell with the name of the ship on it was brought up and displayed to the press but the salvagers would not allow any archaeological assessment of the piece. This led to further speculation as to the authenticity of the artifact.

Ships have been wrecked around Cape Cod for the past three hundred years. The backside between Provincetown and Chatham has been the scene of at least three thousand or more accidents. Ships going aground or being broken up on the outer bars; the toll in the record books is appalling. Several opinions as to the identification of materials recovered at the Wellfleet site have been given. The consensus is that the site is contaminated with many different wrecks and that no positive identification can be ascertained except for findings of period pieces being antique and the coins with dates inscribed. The articles recovered are probably a collection of relics from a large number of vessels which have been wrecked in the same area.

Above: A short circuit in the electrical junction box caused a fire that completely destroyed the fishing vessel *St. Jude* on March 24, 1986, forty miles east of Cape Cod. The Coast Guard brought the crew ashore by helicopter and landed them at the airport in Barnstable. The vessel exploded shortly afterward and sank. *Photo courtesy of the U.S. Coast Guard, Boston, Mass.* **Below:** The 110-foot ketch *Whitehawk* was passing through the Cape Cod Canal in dense fog during the night of August 29, 1986 when she collided with the 641-foot Liberian freighter *Bujin* which was carrying 1,000 automobiles from New York to Boston. Both masts were sheered off, The ketch scratched some paint on the side of the freighter. The hull of the ketch was not damaged but repairs were extensive. *Photo by Renee DeKona, Hyannis, Mass.*

Above: On March 7, 1986, the North Carolina fishing vessel *Sea Rambler* radioed that it was taking on water in heavy seas about 15 miles southwest of Martha's Vineyard at 11 a.m. The Coast Guard launched a helicopter from Air Station Cape Cod. The aircraft arrived in time to lift three crewmen from the vessel. **Below:** The cutter *Vigilant* arrived on scene as the vessel started to sink. *Photos courtesy of the U.S. Coast Guard.*

Above: The *Sea Rambler* sank soon after the arrival of the *Vigilant.* These photos were made by Ken Frederickson, a crewman aboard the cutter. *Photo courtesy of the U.S. Coast Guard.* **Below:** A gasoline barge ran aground near the west end of the Cape Cod Canal on September 17, 1986 and spilled about 25,000 gallons into the waters of Buzzards Bay. The Barge ST-85 hit a rock pile tearing a two-foot wide hole, twenty-five feet long in her hull. The barge Eastern Star was brought alongside the ST-85 and the remaining cargo was pumped aboard. The damaged barge was taken to a shipyard for repairs. *Aerial Photo by Gordon E. Caldwell, Hyannis, Mass.*

Above: The ketch *Calliope* was found on the rocks on Nashawena Island in the Elizabeth Chain on October 4, 1986 laden with about twelve million dollars worth of marijuana. There were no crewmen aboard and the vessel had apparently been abandoned after running aground. The hull was flooded due to several large holes as a result of the grounding. Officials surmise that the previous rough weather had caused the accident. The hull lay on the rocks for several months following the wreck. *Photo by Steve Heaslip, Hyannis, Mass.* **Below:** The *Karie Ann Nicole*, a Portsmouth, N.H. fishing vessel sank about 40 miles northeast of Provincetown on May 3, 1987 after her 3 man crew had abandoned the vessel. They were picked up by another boat and transferred to a Coast Guard cutter. What caused the 42-foot wooden boat to sink was not known. *Photo courtesy of the U.S. Coast Guard.*

What is believed to be the remains of the schooner *Mondego* washed out of the sands of Nauset Beach near the inlet in Orleans. The vessel came ashore in dense fog on March 1, 1900 and was a total loss. The 18 man crew were assisted ashore by the Life Savers. The vessel lay on the beach and her bones had been sanded in until January, 1987. The size of the skeleton is of the right proportions to fit the description of the *Mondego* which helps to support the assumption. *Photo by the Author.*

In late January 1987, what is believed to be the hull of the schooner *Mondego* washed out of the sand near the Nauset inlet and was visible at low tide at the waters edge about a mile north of the bathing beach. On March 1, 1900, the Gloucester fishing vessel stranded on Nauset Beach at 12:15 a.m. in dense fog. The 105 ton vessel lay in the surf near the beach for about an hour before she was discovered by Surfman Snow from the Nauset Station. He immediately telephoned Keeper Alonzo N. Bearse from the watch house to inform him of the grounding.

Keeper Bearse mustered his crew and set out for the wreck. They arrived on the scene at about 2:45 a.m. The schooner at that time was well up on the beach and the Keeper advised the crew to remain on board until the tide ebbed enough to let them come ashore in safety. At about half past three, lines were thrown over the side of the vessel and with the help of the Life Saving crew the eighteen crewmen were brought ashore. Most of the crew walked back to the station for a warm breakfast and some dry clothing. The remainder stayed at the grounded vessel to recover their personal belongings. These men, and the Life Savers, returned to the station at seven in the morning for a hot meal and some needed rest. The schooner *Mondego* was built in 1894 in Essex, Massachusetts. She was 91 feet long with a 23 foot beam and her home port was in Gloucester, Mass. She was only six years old when wrecked on Nauset Beach and her hull was in good condition. The vessel was probably stripped of all useful gear and then buried by tidal action in the Nauset sands. The wreck report stated that the vessel grounded two and one half miles south of the Nauset Station in Eastham and a half mile north of the inlet. The wreckage found, is one half mile south of the inlet in Orleans. A check of chart # 13246 shows that this location checks out exactly 2-1/2 miles south of the Nauset station site. This would indicate that the inlet in 1900 was a mile south of its present location. Some early photographs taken at the site at that time support this finding. The schooner had laid in the sand for 87 years and the lower part of the hull was visible. This is not unusual as parts of the hull of the British frigate *Somerset,* wrecked in Provincetown on Peaked Hill Bars in 1778, are still visible periodically when they wash out of the sands. The exact identification of the *Mondego* is not certain because of the thousands of shipwrecks along the backside of Cape Cod. But the location and the size of the wreckage found helps to support the assumption. John Fish, Director of the Historical Maritime Group of New England, measured the skeleton washed out at the surf line and stated that the wreckage is of the right proportions to fit the description of the schooner *Mondego.*

The Provincetown fishing vessel *Porpoise* sank in March, 1987 after mooring too close to a sand bar in the harbor. The boat stuck on the bar and when the tide came in the vessel filled. The boat was neglected as she lay on the bar and deteriorated. *Photo by the Author.*

GOLD ON THE REPUBLIC

On January 23, 1909, the White Star liner *Republic* was in a collision with the Italian liner *Florida*, fifty miles south of Nantucket Island. The vessel remained afloat for another day. She sank while in tow of U.S. Revenue Cutters for shallow water. After the sinking, the headlines concentrated on the radioman Jack Binns, who had remained at his key sending S.O.S. messages to rescue the 600 passengers on board. The story of the wreck is detailed in Chapter Four. In the years since the vessel sank there have been rumors, reports and stories about a reputed fortune in gold aboard the *Republic.* The amount of the treasure was stated as three million in uncirculated United States gold coins. There are no official U.S. Treasury Department records of a gold shipment aboard the *Republic*; however, the rumors persist. In October 1984, Martin Bayerle, a salvager from Martha's Vineyard announced that he was going to dive on the ship and recover the gold. His claim was based on research he had done on gold shipments out of the country and that a European government had bought the coins from a mint in the United States. Most of the research is based on gold import-export figures and losses declared, the details of which are nebulous. The gold, if it exists and if it is recovered, would have a numismatic value in excess of five-hundred million dollars. Bayerle found the wreck in 260 feet of water in 1981 and was able to identify it positively. He was awarded the salvage rights by the U.S. District Court in Boston.

The actual salvage moved along very slowly as about a million dollars in investment money was required before embarking on so large an effort. But in June, 1986, another group began to dive on the *Republic* and Bayerle failed in court to protect his claim. A New York group of investors had formed a foreign licensed corporation called Marshallton. The lawyers sparred back and forth in court as the salvage effort continued. In July, 1986, the salvagers announced that they had brought up six truckloads of silverware, dishes and various other memorabilia from the vessel. Divers claimed that they found no gold coins on the ship. The materials brought up from the wreck were scheduled to be displayed in a museum at a later date. There is no way to authenticate any of the information reported in the newspapers but any substantial find of treasure would probably not be revealed if it could be kept secret.

Above The fishing vessel *Shearwater* caught fire on May 26, 1987 in Nantucket Sound. One man aboard escaped injury when he was picked up by a sportsman fishing in the area. The Coast Guard sent boats from Chatham and Nantucket to assist in fighting the fire. The vessel was later towed into Saquatucket Harbor in Harwichport on the south side of Cape Cod. *Photo by Steve Heaslip, Hyannis, Mass.* **Below:** The fishing vessel Carole L. ran aground on Great Point, Nantucket on August 22, 1987. The Coast Guard aided the crew but the boat could not be saved. Heavy seas broke up the hull a few days later. *Photo by PA2 Gregory Creedon, U.S. Coast Guard, Boston, Mass.*

Three helicopters from Air Station Cape Cod participated in a spectacular rescue 210 miles out into the Atlantic on March 14, 1987, when a Soviet freighter, the *Komsomolets Kirgizii* sent out a distress call. The vessel had drifted into the trough of the waves after the engines stopped and the cargo shifted. The first helicopter rescued 15 persons from the stricken ship. The second chopped lifted 16 and the final aircraft picked up the remaining 6 including the Captain. *Photos courtesy of the U.S. Coast Guard.*

The total persons rescued numbered 37 and the ship sank soon after the rescue. The crew of the vessel, shown in one of the helicopters, were landed at the F.A.A. Technical Center at Pamona, New Jersey. The following week, the crew of the Soviet ship and the rescue crews from Otis were invited to the White House at Washington. President Reagan pinned medals on the Coast Guard crews. *Photo courtesy of the U.S. Coast Guard.*

Above: On November 26, 1987 the 300 foot container barge Boston Patriot was cast ashore on the Sandwich beach after it broke loose from its tugboat during high winds just after clearing the Cape Cod Canal. The barge had to be unloaded to free her from the sand. Bad weather delayed the operations until mid December. **Below:** A large crane on a salvage barge was brought to the area and unloaded the containers onto other barges. The Boston Patriot was pulled off on December 23rd and towed to Boston. Damage was limited to some holes in the bottom made by the rocks on the beach. *Aerial Photos by the Author.*

Above: The New Bedford fishing vessel *Trade Wind* sank in the West End of the Cape Cod Canal on May 6, 1988. She had apparently hit some rocks on her passage through the waterway and sank near the State Pier. The vessel lay on the bottom for six days until salvagers pumped her out and towed her to her home port. Damage was at a minimum. **Below:** Stormy weather sank the dredge Herring II at the entrance to Sesuit Harbor in Dennis on June 2, 1988. The vessel leaked a quantity of fuel oil and north winds carried the oil into the harbor and onto the shellfish beds in Sesuit Creek. A professional hazardous waste company cleaned up the spill and the dredge was refloated. *Photos by the Author.*

Above: On the night of October 20, 1987, the Gloucester fishing boat *Toots* ran aground attempting to navigate the new break through in Chatham. The new cut is very dangerous in rough water and inexperienced fishermen have been caught at various times but, to date, no serious losses have been recorded. **Below:** A close up view of the vessel laying on the sands. The *Toots* was pulled off on the 23rd by another Chatham fishing boat. *Aerial Photos by the Author.*

Above: Early in the morning of August 22, 1988, the small sloop Doe ran aground on Nauset outer beach three miles south of the town parking lot. The boat was not damaged. A private tug pulled the small sailboat off the beach on the next high tide. *Aerial photo by the Author.* **Below:** The fishing boat *Nancy Christine II* ran aground in Woods Hole, on August 5, 1988. The western rig trawler lay over on her side when the tide went out. The crew escaped without injuries. The boat was salvaged the next day by a New Bedford salvage company. *Photo by Stephen Rose.*

A construction barge broke loose from its mooring in Provincetown Harbor on October 22, 1988. The barge was blown ashore by 50-mile-an-hour winds. Damage was at a minimum and the barge was towed off the beach a couple days later. *Photo by the Author.*

Above: The latest addition to the U.S. Coast Guard on the water and in the air is the "Famous" class cutters, named for another previous cutter prominent in Coast Guard History. There are thirteen 270-foot medium endurance vessels used in search and rescue, marine science, defense operations and coastal surveillance. The number 905 is on the *U.S.S. Spencer,* stationed in Boston, Mass. **Below:** The Coast Guard recently added 96 short range HH-65A helicopters to its fleet to replace the old HH-52A flying lifeboats. The new choppers are used in all the missions of search and rescue, law enforcement, polar ice breaking and pollution control. The twin engine "Dolphins" operate up to 150 miles off shore and will fly at 150 knots for three hours. The shrouded tail rotor is unique to this aircraft.

Above: The Wellfleet fishing vessel *Patricia J.* on the Brewster flats after running aground on March 24, 1989. Her skipper, Paul Gensler of Wellfleet had apparently fell overboard while shellfishing in Cape Cod Bay. He was fishing alone at the time and no one witnessed the tragedy. Friends and relatives tried unsuccessfully to save the vessel as she lay, tilted on the flats at low tide. The fishing vessel was a total loss. *Photo by John Leaning.* **Below:**The Steamship Authority vessel *Eagle* ran aground on a sand bar in Lewis Bay, just outside Hyannis on June 30, 1989 about two o'clock in the afternoon. The ship was aground for three hours when it pulled off by a tugboat. There were no injuries among the 218 passengers aboard, nor any reports of oil spilled by the grounding. The delay caused a sticky back-up in summer traffic on the boatline. *Photo by Steve Heaslip.*

Above: On October 22, 1989, the barge COLUMBIA went aground off Wings Neck in Pocasset after a tow line from the tug *Harriet Moran* parted. The two was enroute from Boston to New Jersey when the cable broke early in the morning. The barge was on the rocks for about twelve hours before it was pulled off by three tugs. Divers inspected the hull and found no damage. The barge was then towed to her original destination. *Photo by Sherwood Landers.* **Below:** Small fishing boats are wrecked on the backside of Cape Cod frequetly. Only the hull is left after the salvage crews are finished. These hulks become playgounds for the local youngsters on the beach in the summer months. Note the hole in the after part of the hull and the cut section at the top of the bow. The engine was removed by the easiest way and the name of the boat was cut out with a chain saw. *Photo by the Author.*

The Coast Guard wages a never ending battle with the elements in their quest improved search and rescue techniques. One of the latest in small craft is the "Hurricane", a 21-foot rigid hull inflatable with a Volvo Penta inboard-outboard engine. These photographs were taken at the new Chatham cut-through with Chief Jack Downey, BM1 Kyle Santheson and Capt. Peter Collom of the First Coast Guard District. They put the boat through its paces in some rough water opposite the Chatham Station. *First Coast Guard District photos.*

The new Hurricane, above, is contrasted with one of the old lifeboats from the Nauset Station in Eastham pictured below. The speed of answering a rescue call is enhanced with a high powered craft, against the slow launch and recover of the life-boat using oars. The men pulling were able to rescue many of those whose lives were in peril but with a fraction of the efficiency of the modern day coastal vanguards.

Above: The 62-foot New Bedford dragger *Linda & Stephanie* came ashore at Newcomb Hollow Beach, late in the evening of November 8, 1989. The fishing net fouled the propeller and stalled the engine. An fresh east wind caused the boat to go ashore. **Below:** When the tide dropped, local officials monitored the situation as the crew cleared the propeller. The fishing vessel was pulled off the next day by a commercial tugboat. *Photos by Gordon E. Caldwell.*

The study of shipwrecks around Cape Cod is an intriguing subject. The variety of accidents over the past century and more maintains the interest and fascination for maritime scholars and marine buffs. The storms will continue to take their toll but modern technology is improving the lot of the sailor and his vessel. The ships, however, are operated by man and human error will contribute to the number of accidents as it always has. The sea has not seen the last of the sailing ships. The known energy sources to propel vessels are being used up and the day will come when man may return to the wind for power. The methods will be different but the results will be the same, as modern science and computers collaborate on designs and construction. Today, man is solving the mysteries of the ocean depths. Tomorrow's sailor may see the day when a shipwreck is but a memory of the past. That day, however, may be many centuries in the future.

Another unidentified fishing boat ashore in Provincetown. This event occurrs frequently and is usually corrected on the next high tide. The main cause is getting lost in the fog and running up on the beach. When the surf is light damage to the hull is negligible. *Photo by Neal Nickerson, Provincetown, Mass.*

ACKNOWLEDGEMENTS

During the collection of photographs and assembly of this volume, several people have been instrumental in assisting with the loan of pictures and information. Many more have helped me with research and development. In addition to those whose names appear in the credit lines, there are others who assisted with accurate information about disasters and made other contributions to the book. They are: Arnie Carr, John Fish, Bob Beattie, Dick Boonisar, Charlie Sayle, Connie Driscoll, John Lochhead, Joseph A. Nickerson, Clive Driver, Noel Beyle, Ken Black, Greg Creeden-U.S.C.G., Fred Thompson, Frank Claes, Mary Clark, Harold Jennings, Barry Homer, Gordon E. Caldwell, Richard Griggs, Coast Guard Historian Robert Scheina, John Ullman, the late Richard C. Kelsey, and my artist-historian friend Paul C. Morris. I wish to thank the Libraries of the several museums listed in the bibliography for allowing me access to their photo banks. And to those who allowed me to copy their family photographs from collections for inclusion in this book. Many kind thanks to all.

W.P.Q.

BIBLIOGRAPHY

Mooncussers of Cape Cod by Henry C. Kitteridge
The Pirates of the New England Coast, 1630-1730 by Dow & Edmonds
History of Barnstable County by Simeon Deyo
Wrecks Around Nantucket 1664-1915 by Arthur H. Gardner
The Humane Society of Massachusetts 1785-1916 by Howe
Report of Ship Canal, 1864, Comm. of Mass.
The Cape Cod Canal by Robert H. Farson
Cape Cod Historical Almanac by Donald G. Trayser
Lore of the Wreckers by Birse Shepard
American Sailing Coasters of the No. Atlantic by Paul C. Morris
Four Masted Schooners of the East Coast by Paul C. Morris
Schooners and Schooner Barges by Paul C. Morris
The Island Steamers by Morris & Morin
Lightships of Cape Cod by Frederic L. Thompson
Marconi Wireless on Cape Cod by Michael E. Whatley
Shipwrecks on Martha's Vineyard by Dorothy R. Scoville
Rum War at Sea by Malcolm F. Willoughby
The Great Coal Schooners of New England by Capt. W.J.L. Parker
The Target Ship in Cape Cod Bay by Noel W. Beyle
United States Life Saving Service Reports
United States Lighthouse Board Reports
U.S. List of Merchant Vessels

Newspapers:

The Cape Cod Independent
The New Bedford Standard Times
The Cape Cod Standard Times
The Cape Codder
The New York Times
The Bath Daily News

Museums & Historical Societies

The Mariners Museum, Newport News, Virginia
The Peabody Museum of Salem, Salem, Massachusetts
The Fall River Marine Museum, Fall River, Massachusetts
The Bath Marine Museum, Bath, Maine
Steamship Historical Society Library, Baltimore, Maryland
Mystic Seaport Museum, Mystic, Connecticut

Shipwrecks are rare today on the beaches of Cape Cod. Space age navigation helps reduce the groundings. The beaches today show other types of activity. When sports fishermen travel down the shores in vehicles with large tires, they make interesting and varying patterns in the sands. *Aerial Photo by the Author.*